THE POET AT PLAY

KALLIMACHOS, THE BATH OF PALLAS

MNEMOSYNE

BIBLIOTHECA CLASSICA BATAVA

COLLEGERUNT

B. A. VAN GRONINGEN, W. J. VERDENIUS, J. H. WASZINK

BIBLIOTHECAE AB ACTIS FUIT FASCICULOSQUE
EDENDOS CURAVIT W. J. VERDENIUS, HOMERUSLAAN 53, ZEIST

SUPPLEMENTUM SEXTUM

K. J. Mc Kay, The Poet at Play

LUGDUNI BATAVORUM E. J. BRILL 1962

THE POET AT PLAY

KALLIMACHOS, THE BATH OF PALLAS

BY

K. J. Mc KAY

Senior Lecturer in Classical Studies, University of Melbourne

LEIDEN
E. J. BRILL
1962

The costs of publication of this study have been assisted by a generous grant from the Publications Committee of the University of Melbourne.

PRINTED IN THE NETHERLANDS

TABLE OF CONTENTS

PREFACE

Kallimachos was not by nature a poet who encouraged familiarity, and lapse of time, which has turned so many works, acknowledged in their day as masterpieces, into glittering or, more often, dull fragments, has tended to make this poet's work more inscrutable still. And yet his finest poems were not intended to be private revelations. The discerning were invited to pass judgment on his poetry, only 'by its art, not by the Persian furlong'. At the present day the shortage of introductory studies eloquently testifies to our inability to make the most of this invitation. If few read his Hymns today, it is because few have felt in a position to offer them guidance.

It is worth recalling what we have of recent date. For text we are well served by R. Pfeiffer, *Callimachus* vol. II (Oxford 1953). Cruces remain, but we shall always be in Professor Pfeiffer's debt. For exegesis there is only E. Cahen's *Les hymnes de Callimaque* (Paris 1930), which leaves much to be desired and is now out of print. Perhaps I should add P. A. Ardizzoni's *Gl'inni di Callimaco* (Catania Stud. Edit. Mod. 1932), which I have not seen. A comprehensive commentary on the Hymns still remains to be written, but it is my own opinion that we are not yet ready for it. Regrettably, there is no study in English of any hymn, and authors of handbooks on Greek literature are inclined to translate into elegant verse and leave the reader to assess the worth of their generalizations for himself. Undoubtedly some have need to take to heart the trenchant criticism of J. P. Elder: 'The incense and holy-water school of literary criticism which rejoices in a well-bred "charming" and forbids dissection neither educates nor stimulates'. Others write in terms which deter the student even from finding out for himself.

The enquiring searcher for the facts is at present most likely to turn to an edition which provides some pabulum in the form of introduction, translation and notes. A. W. Mair's edition in the Loeb series dates from 1921, and includes only a page or so of comment on each poem. E. Cahen's edition in the French Budé series, first produced in 1922 and kept alive by minor transfusions (4th. edition by A. Puech-P. Mazon, 1953), has more pages to spare, but uses them badly. The Swiss edition of E. Howald and E. Staiger

(Artemis Verlag: Zürich, 1955) is modern and sensitive, but their introductory studies are anchored to the viewpoint expressed in Howald's *Der Dichter Kallimachos von Kyrene* (1943), with which I express my disagreement in Chapter V. To be sure, they are all victims of the limitations imposed by publishers of Classical series. Kallimachos has everything to lose from this situation, for his secrets rarely become apparent at the first reading.

Above all there is cause for regret in the absence of commentaries upon Hymns 5 and 6. 'Die beiden letzten .. zuerst die ganz eigene Kunst dieses Dichters leuchten lassen' [1]; they belong 'den vollendetsten Schöpfungen des Dichters' [2]. They are also hymns in which Kallimachos subordinates all the much maligned tricks of Hellenistic poetry to a careful plan, and serve as a good introduction to the poet's skill.

It will be obvious to every scholar that the man who prepares an interpretation of a Callimachean hymn, with the needs of the student in mind, has not such a mass of widely accepted material at his disposal that he can avoid defending a new thesis. Perhaps it should be foreshadowed now. I am suggesting that Kallimachos, attracted by a primitive version of the Teiresias story, set out to explain it in the context of the Argive cult of Athene Oxyderkes (and, as a pendant, Doric threnodic elegy); that in H. 6 the poet depicts another mood of Doric, namely comedy, with Epicharmos especially in mind. The ingenuity which in H. 5 is displayed in arranging the connexions with Athene Oxyderkes, in H. 6 is apparent in the treatment of the Erysichthon story. Later I shall develop this last point in a study of the use made of Erysichthon in Classical literature.

I count it, in a way, fortunate that I had formulated my ideas before I had an opportunity of reading H. Kleinknecht's long study of the Fifth Hymn in *Hermes* 74 (1939), 301-350 (published at the outbreak of war and hard to find in this country). This learned *Habilitationschrift*, which contains valuable illustrative material, gave me an opportunity to test my theory. If it has been strengthened by the comparison, I am also sure that it has been enriched.

I should emphasize that this is not an edition, but an interpretation, of the Fifth Hymn. The scholar will notice omissions but, I trust, of no major item which contributes to an appreciation of the

---

[1]   Wilamowitz, *Hellenistische Dichtung*, I p. 182.
[2]   Howald-Staiger, p.134.

poet's talents. To save tedious reference to another work I have included a text (which, except in two places, is the same as Pfeiffer's) and prose translation [1]. The latter lays no claim to literary merit, but is simply a guide to my interpretation of key lines. I despair of an adequate translation in either prose or verse. Let those who would disagree consider the *sonority* of even such a line as H. 5.79; I hope that they will then understand.

I have written proper names in a Greek form because I feel that we need to be reminded that Kallimachos is an artist in his own right, not merely a precursory *poeta nouus*. At the same time, I have tried not to do much violence to conventional pronunciation (hence Kallimachos, but Cyrene). I cannot, however, claim to have been consistent. A special problem was the fact that often questions of function, feeling, dialect and metre are involved in gauging the total effect of a given line, but these questions had to be treated in separate chapters. As a result there has been some unavoidable cross referencing, but the indices have been designed to draw the threads together.

I have assumed acquaintance with a general article such as that in the Oxford Classical Dictionary.

The title is a tribute to a stimulating chapter of Bruno Snell's *Die Entdeckung des Geistes*[3] (1955), pp. 353-370 (*Discovery of the Mind*, trans. T. G. Rosenmeyer, 1953, pp. 264-280). Lastly, I dedicate my work to my wife, in gratitude for her patience before an enthusiasm which she could not share, and for her faith which lightened a difficult task.

Melbourne, November 1960. K. J. Mc KAY

---

[1] I decided against providing Chapter VI with a text or complete translation of Hymn 6, for defence of my readings and interpretations would prove too much of a distraction. Mair's translation will be adequate for the context of that chapter.

LIST OF ABBREVIATIONS

A. f. RW.	Archiv für Religionswissenschaft
A. J. A.	American Journal of Archaeology
A. J. Ph.	American Journal of Philology
B. C. H.	Bulletin de Correspondence Hellénique
C. Ph.	Classical Philology
C. Q.	Classical Quarterly
C. R.	Classical Review
E. R. E.	J. Hastings' Encyclopaedia of Religion and Ethics
Herm.	Hermes
H. S. C. Ph.	Harvard Studies in Classical Philology
I. G.	Inscriptiones Graecae (Berlin, 1873-)
J. H. S.	Journal of Hellenic Studies
Mnem.	Mnemosyne
M. S. L.	Mémoires de la Société de Linguistique
Mus. Helv.	Museum Helveticum
N. Jbb.	Neue Jahrbücher für das klassischen Altertum
P. Oxy.	Oxyrhynchus Papyri
Philol.	Philologus
R. E.	Pauly-Wissowa-Kroll, Real-Encyclopädie
R. E. A.	Revue des Études Anciennes
R. E. G.	Revue des Études Grecques
Rh. Mus.	Rheinisches Museum
T. A. P. A.	Transactions of the American Philological Association
Wien. Stud.	Wiener Studien

Cahen's *Callimaque et son œuvre poétique* and *Les hymnes de Callimaque* are respectively referred to as Cahen, *Callimaque* and Cahen, *Comm(entaire)*. Kleinknecht (generally with a page reference) refers to his article in *Hermes* 74 (1939), 301-350.

THE POET AT PLAY
KALLIMACHOS, THE BATH OF PALLAS

ΕΙΣ ΛΟΥΤΡΑ ΤΗΣ ΠΑΛΛΑΔΟΣ

Ὅσσαι λωτροχόοι τᾶς Παλλάδος ἔξιτε πᾶσαι,
   ἔξιτε· τᾶν ἵππων ἄρτι φρυασσομενᾶν
τᾶν ἱερᾶν ἐσάκουσα, καὶ ἁ θεὸς εὔτυκος ἕρπεν·
   σοῦσθέ νυν, ὦ ξανθαὶ σοῦσθε Πελασγιάδες.
οὔποκ' Ἀθαναία μεγάλως ἀπενίψατο πάχεις,   5
   πρὶν κόνιν ἱππειᾶν ἐξελάσαι λαγόνων·
οὐδ' ὅκα δὴ λύθρῳ πεπαλαγμένα πάντα φέροισα
   τεύχεα τῶν ἀδίκων ἦνθ' ἀπὸ γαγενέων,
ἀλλὰ πολὺ πράτιστον ὑφ' ἅρματος αὐχένας ἵππων
   λυσαμένα παγαῖς ἔκλυσεν Ὠκεανῶ   10
ἱδρῶ καὶ ῥαθάμιγγας, ἐφοίβασεν δὲ παγέντα
   πάντα χαλινοφάγων ἀφρὸν ἀπὸ στομάτων.
ὦ ἴτ' Ἀχαιιάδες, καὶ μὴ μύρα μηδ' ἀλαβάστρως
   (συρίγγων ἀΐω φθόγγον ὑπαξονίων),
μὴ μύρα λωτροχόοι τᾷ Παλλάδι μηδ' ἀλαβάστρως   15
   (οὐ γὰρ Ἀθαναία χρίματα μεικτὰ φιλεῖ)
οἴσετε μηδὲ κάτοπτρον· ἀεὶ καλὸν ὄμμα τὸ τήνας.
   οὐδ' ὅκα τὰν Ἴδᾳ Φρὺξ ἐδίκαζεν ἔριν,
οὔτ' ἐς ὀρείχαλκον μεγάλα θεὸς οὔτε Σιμοῦντος
   ἔβλεψεν δίναν ἐς διαφαινομέναν·   20
οὐδ' Ἥρα· Κύπρις δὲ διαυγέα χαλκὸν ἑλοῖσα
   πολλάκι τὰν αὐτὰν δὶς μετέθηκε κόμαν.
ἁ δὲ δὶς ἑξήκοντα διαθρέξασα διαύλως,
   οἷα παρ' Εὐρώτᾳ τοὶ Λακεδαιμόνιοι
ἀστέρες, ἐμπεράμως ἐτρίψατο λιτὰ βαλοῖσα   25
   χρίματα, τᾶς ἰδίας ἔκγονα φυταλιᾶς,
ὦ κῶραι, τὸ δ' ἔρευθος ἀνέδραμε, πρώιον οἵαν
   ἢ ῥόδον ἢ σίβδας κόκκος ἔχει χροΐαν.
τῷ καὶ νῦν ἄρσεν τι κομίσσατε μῶνον ἔλαιον,
   ᾧ Κάστωρ, ᾧ καὶ χρίεται Ἡρακλέης·   30
οἴσετε καὶ κτένα οἱ παγχρύσεον, ὡς ἀπὸ χαίταν
   πέξηται, λιπαρὸν σμασαμένα πλόκαμον.
ἔξιθ', Ἀθαναία· πάρα τοι καταθύμιος ἵλα,
   παρθενικαὶ μεγάλων παῖδες Ἀρεστοριδᾶν·
ὠθάνα, φέρεται δὲ καὶ ἁ Διομήδεος ἀσπίς,   35
   ὡς ἔθος Ἀργείως τοῦτο παλαιοτέρως

THE BATH OF PALLAS

Process, all you who attend Pallas at her bath, process! I hear just now the sacred horses whinnying! The goddess too is ready to come! Come hasten, fair daughters of Pelasgos, hasten! Never did Athene wash her mighty arms before driving away the dust from her horses' flanks, not even when she returned from battle with the lawless Giants, her armour all befouled with gore; but first of all she freed her horses' necks from her chariot and bathed off the drops of sweat in the springs of Ocean, and washed away all the clotted foam from their mouths that champed the bit.

Proceed, Achaean maids, but no perfumes or alabaster vials (I hear the sound of the axle-naves!), no perfumes or alabaster vials for Pallas, attendants at her bath, (for Athene has no liking for compounded ointments) are you to bring, nor mirror either. She is always fair of sight. Not even when the Phrygian judged the famous dispute on Ida did the mighty goddess look into either mirror of orichalc or the transparent eddy of Simois; nor Hera either. But Aphrodite took a shining mirror of bronze and many times adjusted and re-adjusted the same curl. While Pallas, after a run of twice sixty double circuits of the racetrack, like the stars of Sparta by the Eurotas, skilfully applied simple ointments, girls, the product of her own plant, and rubbed herself. And a ruddy glow flared up, like the colour of an early rose or pomegranate seed. Hence on this occasion bring only manly olive oil, with which Kastor, and Herakles too, anoint themselves. Bring also a comb all of gold for her, so that she may comb her hair when she has anointed her gleaming tresses.

Process, Athene! A congenial company is here for you, the maiden daughters of Arestor's mighty sons. And, Athene, the shield of Diomedes also is being brought, as Eumedes, your favourite priest,

Εὐμήδης ἐδίδαξε, τεῒν κεχαρισμένος ἱρεύς·
ὃς ποκα βωλευτὸν γνοὺς ἐπί οἱ θάνατον
δᾶμον ἑτοιμάζοντα φυγᾷ τεὸν ἱρὸν ἄγαλμα
   ᾤχετ' ἔχων, Κρεῖον δ' εἰς ὄρος ᾠκίσατο,   40
Κρεῖον ὄρος· σὲ δέ, δαῖμον, ἀπορρώγεσσιν ἔθηκεν
   ἐν πέτραις, αἷς νῦν οὔνομα Παλλατίδες.
ἔξιθ', Ἀθαναία περσέπτολι, χρυσεοπήληξ,
   ἵππων καὶ σακέων ἀδομένα πατάγῳ.
σάμερον, ὑδροφόροι, μὴ βάπτετε — σάμερον, Ἄργος,   45
   πίνετ' ἀπὸ κρανᾶν μηδ' ἀπὸ τῶ ποταμῶ·
σάμερον αἱ δῶλαι τὰς κάλπιδας ἢ 'ς Φυσάδειαν
   ἢ ἐς Ἀμυμώναν οἴσετε τὰν Δαναῶ.
καὶ γὰρ δὴ χρυσῷ τε καὶ ἄνθεσιν ὕδατα μείξας
   ἡξεῖ φορβαίων Ἴναχος ἐξ ὀρέων   50
τἀθάνᾳ τὸ λοετρὸν ἄγων καλόν. ἀλλά, Πελασγέ,
   φράζεο μὴ οὐκ ἐθέλων τὰν βασίλειαν ἴδῃς.
ὅς κεν ἴδῃ γυμνὰν τὰν Παλλάδα τὰν πολιοῦχον,
   τὦργος ἐσοψεῖται τοῦτο πανυστάτιον.
πότνι' Ἀθαναία, σὺ μὲν ἔξιθι· μέσφα δ' ἐγώ τι   55
   ταῖσδ' ἐρέω· μῦθος δ' οὐκ ἐμός, ἀλλ' ἑτέρων.
παῖδες, Ἀθαναία νύμφαν μίαν ἔν ποκα Θήβαις
   πουλύ τι καὶ πέρι δὴ φίλατο τᾶν ἑταρᾶν,
ματέρα Τειρεσίαο, καὶ οὔποκα χωρὶς ἔγεντο·
   ἀλλὰ καὶ ἀρχαίων εὖτ' ἐπὶ Θεσπιέων   60
⟨ἢ 'πι Πλαταιάων⟩ [1] ἢ εἰς Ἁλίαρτον ἐλαύνοι
   ἵππως, Βοιωτῶν ἔργα διερχομένα,
ἢ 'πὶ Κορωνείας, ἵνα οἱ τεθυωμένον ἄλσος
   καὶ βωμοὶ ποταμῷ κεῖντ' ἐπὶ Κουραλίῳ,
πολλάκις ἀ δαίμων νιν ἑῶ ἐπεβάσατο δίφρω,   65
   οὐδ' ὄαροι νυμφᾶν οὐδὲ χοροστασίαι
ἀδεῖαι τελέθεσκον, ὅκ' οὐχ ἁγεῖτο Χαρικλώ·
   ἀλλ' ἔτι καὶ τήναν δάκρυα πόλλ' ἔμενε,
καίπερ Ἀθαναίᾳ καταθύμιον ἔσσαν ἑταίραν.
   δή ποκα γὰρ πέπλων λυσαμένα περόνας   70
ἵππω ἐπὶ κράνᾳ Ἑλικωνίδι καλὰ ῥεοίσᾳ
   λῶντο· μεσαμβρινὰ δ' εἶχ' ὄρος ἀσυχία.
ἀμφότεραι λώοντο, μεσαμβριναὶ δ' ἔσαν ὦραι,

---

[1] I follow Howald-Staiger in restoring P. Bernadini Marzolla's suggestion
(*Stud. Ital. Fil. Class.* 26 (1952), 211 f.), based on Nonn. *Dion.* 4.335 ff. and
13.70 f.

taught this custom to the Argives of olden days. Who once, learning that the people were preparing a scheme to kill him, fled with your sacred image and settled on Mt. Kreion, yes, Mt. Kreion. And you, goddess, he placed on the precipitous crags which now bear the name of Pallatides.

Process, Athene, Sacker of Cities, lady of the golden casque, who delights in the clash of horse and shield. Today, water carrier, do not dip—today, Argos, drink from the springs and not from the river—today, servants, bring your pitchers to Physadeia or Amymone, Danaos' child. For Inachos, covering his waters with gold and flowers, will come from the fertile mountains, bringing the finest of baths for Athene. But, Argive, take care lest unwittingly you behold the Queen. Whoever sees Pallas, Guardian of the City, naked, he shall see this Argos for the very last time.

Lady Athene, do you process; and meantime I shall tell a tale to these girls, not my own, but the tale of others.

Girls, once in Thebes Athene loved a nymph dearly, her special favourite among her companions. She was the mother of Teiresias and they were always inseparable. Even when Athene drove her team towards ancient Thespiai, towards Plataiai or to Haliartos, traversing the ploughland of Boeotia, or towards Koroneia, where her fragrant grove and altars are situated by the river Kuralios, often she placed the nymph beside her in the chariot; nor were the conversations and dances of the nymphs agreeable to her unless Chariklo was taking the lead in them. But many a tear still awaited even her, although a companion congenial to Athene.

For once, loosing the brooches of their dresses, they were bathing in Hippokrene, the fair flowing spring of Helikon; and noontide calm possessed the mountain. Both were at their bath, and it was the noontide hour, and a deep calm possessed that mountain. But

πολλὰ δ' ἀσυχία τῆνο κατεῖχεν ὄρος.
Τειρεσίας δ' ἔτι μῶνος ἁμᾶ κυσὶν ἄρτι γένεια 75
  περκάζων ἱερὸν χῶρον ἀνεστρέφετο·
διψάσας δ' ἄφατόν τι ποτὶ ῥόον ἤλυθε κράνας,
  σχέτλιος· οὐκ ἐθέλων δ' εἶδε τὰ μὴ θεμιτά.
τὸν δὲ χολωσαμένα περ ὅμως προσέφασεν Ἀθάνα·
  'τίς σε, τὸν ὀφθαλμὼς οὐκέτ' ἀποισόμενον, 80
ὦ Εὐηρείδα, χαλεπὰν ὁδὸν ἄγαγε δαίμων;'
  ἁ μὲν ἔφα, παιδὸς δ' ὄμματα νὺξ ἔλαβεν.
ἑστάκη δ' ἄφθογγος, ἐκόλλασαν γὰρ ἀνῖαι
  γώνατα καὶ φωνὰν ἔσχεν ἀμαχανία.
ἁ νύμφα δ' ἐβόασε· 'τί μοι τὸν κῶρον ἔρεξας 85
  πότνια; τοιαῦται, δαίμονες, ἐστὲ φίλαι;
ὄμματά μοι τῶ παιδὸς ἀφείλεο. τέκνον ἄλαστε,
  εἶδες Ἀθαναίας στήθεα καὶ λαγόνας,
ἀλλ' οὐκ ἀέλιον πάλιν ὄψεαι. ὦ ἐμὲ δειλάν,
  ὦ ὄρος, ὦ Ἑλικὼν οὐκέτι μοι παριτέ, 90
ἦ μεγάλ' ἀντ' ὀλίγων ἐπράξαο· δόρκας ὀλέσσας
  καὶ πρόκας οὐ πολλὰς φάεα παιδὸς ἔχεις.'
ἁ μὲν <ἄμ'> ἀμφοτέραισι φίλον περὶ παῖδα λαβοῖσα
  μάτηρ μὲν γοερὰν οἶτον ἀηδονίδων
ἆγε βαρὺ κλαίοισα, θεὰ δ' ἐλέησεν ἑταίραν. 95
  καὶ νιν Ἀθαναία πρὸς τόδ' ἔλεξεν ἔπος·
'δῖα γύναι, μετὰ πάντα βαλεῦ πάλιν ὅσσα δι' ὀργάν
  εἶπας· ἐγὼ δ' οὔ τοι τέκνον ἔθηκ' ἀλαόν.
οὐ γὰρ Ἀθαναίᾳ γλυκερὸν πέλει ὄμματα παίδων
  ἁρπάζειν· Κρόνιοι δ' ὧδε λέγοντι νόμοι· 100
ὅς κε τιν' ἀθανάτων, ὅκα μὴ θεὸς αὐτὸς ἕληται,
  ἀθρήσῃ, μισθῶ τοῦτον ἰδεῖν μεγάλω.
δῖα γύναι, τὸ μὲν οὐ παλινάγρετον αὖθι γένοιτο
  ἔργον, ἐπεὶ Μοιρᾶν ὧδ' ἐπένησε λίνα,
ἁνίκα τὸ πρᾶτόν νιν ἐγείναο· νῦν δὲ κομίζευ 105
  ὦ Εὐηρείδα, τέλθος ὀφειλόμενον.
πόσσα μὲν ἁ Καδμηὶς ἐς ὕστερον ἔμπυρα καυσεῖ,
  πόσσα δ' Ἀρισταῖος, τὸν μόνον εὐχόμενοι
παῖδα, τὸν ἁβατὰν Ἀκταίονα, τυφλὸν ἰδέσθαι.
  καὶ τῆνος μεγάλας σύνδρομος Ἀρτέμιδος 110
ἔσσεται· ἀλλ' οὐκ αὐτὸν ὅ τε δρόμος αἵ τ' ἐν ὄρεσσι
  ῥυσεῦνται ξυναὶ τᾶμος ἑκαβολίαι,
ὁππόταν οὐκ ἐθέλων περ ἴδῃ χαρίεντα λοετρά

Teiresias, still an only child, his chin just now darkening with down, was ranging with his dogs the holy place. With an indescribable thirst he came to the flowing spring, poor wretch. Against his will he saw what is not lawful to be seen. But despite her anger Athene nonetheless addressed him: 'What spirit, son of Everes, brought you on this troublesome journey, never to take away your eyes?' So she spoke, and night seized the lad's eyes.

He stood speechless, for pain glued his knees and helplessness gripped his voice. But the nymph shrieked: 'What have you done to my son, lady? Goddesses, is this the sort of friends that you are? You have taken away the eyes of my son. Wretched child, you saw the breasts and flanks of Athene, but you shall not see the sun again. O my misery, O mountain, O Helikon which I may never cross again, you have exacted great things in return for small; having lost a few roe and deer you hold the eyes of my son.'

And at the same time his mother embraced her dear son, and tearfully raised the heavy plaint of the mournful nightingales. Divine Athene took pity on her companion and addressed to her these words: 'Noble lady, take back again all that you have said in anger. I did not make your child blind, for it is not pleasing to Athene to rob lads of their eyes. But thus state the laws of Kronos: "Whoever sees one of the immortals at a moment not of the divinity's choosing, must pay dearly for the sight". Noble lady, this act cannot be reversed again, for so span the Fates' thread from the first moment that you gave him birth. Now receive, O son of Everes, the debt that is owed to you.

How many sacrifices shall the daughter of Kadmos later burn, how many sacrifices Aristaios, praying to see blind their only son, young Aktaion. And he will course with mighty Artemis; but their coursing and common feats of archery on the mountains shall not save him when, although unwitting, he sees the goddess's lovely

δαίμονος· ἀλλ' αὐταὶ τὸν πρὶν ἄνακτα κύνες
τουτάκι δειπνησεῦντι· τὰ δ' υἱέος ὀστέα μάτηρ   115
    λεξεῖται δρυμὼς πάντας ἐπερχομένα·
ὀλβίσταν δ' ἐρέει σε καὶ εὐαίωνα γενέσθαι
    ἐξ ὀρέων ἀλαὸν παῖδ' ὑποδεξαμέναν.
ὦ ἑτάρα, τῷ μή τι μινύρεο· τῷδε γὰρ ἄλλα
    τεῦ χάριν ἐξ ἐμέθεν πολλὰ μενεῦντι γέρα,   120
μάντιν ἐπεὶ θησῶ νιν ἀοίδιμον ἐσσομένοισιν,
    ἦ μέγα τῶν ἄλλων δή τι περισσότερον.
γνωσεῖται δ' ὄρνιχας, ὃς αἴσιος οἵ τε πέτονται
    ἤλιθα καὶ ποίων οὐκ ἀγαθαὶ πτέρυγες.
πολλὰ δὲ Βοιωτοῖσι θεοπρόπα, πολλὰ δὲ Κάδμῳ   125
    χρησεῖ, καὶ μεγάλοις ὕστερα Λαβδακίδαις.
δωσῶ καὶ μέγα βάκτρον, ὅ οἱ πόδας ἐς δέον ἀξεῖ,
    δωσῶ καὶ βιότω τέρμα πολυχρόνιον,
καὶ μόνος, εὖτε θάνῃ, πεπνυμένος ἐν νεκύεσσι
    φοιτασεῖ, μεγάλῳ τίμιος Ἁγεσίλᾳ.'   130
ὣς φαμένα κατένευσε· τὸ δ' ἐντελές, ᾧ κ' ἐπινεύσῃ
    Παλλάς, ἐπεὶ μώνᾳ Ζεὺς τόγε θυγατέρων
δῶκεν Ἀθαναίᾳ πατρώια πάντα φέρεσθαι.
    λωτροχόοι, μάτηρ δ' οὔτις ἔτικτε θεάν,
ἀλλὰ Διὸς κορυφά. κορυφὰ Διὸς οὐκ ἐπινεύει   135
    ψεύδεα   αι θυγάτηρ.
ἔρχετ' Ἀθαναία νῦν ἀτρεκές· ἀλλὰ δέχεσθε
    τὰν θεόν, ὦ κῶραι, τὦργον ὅσαις μέλεται,
σύν τ' εὐαγορίᾳ σύν τ' εὔγμασι σύν τ' ὀλολυγαῖς.
    χαῖρε, θεά, κάδευ δ' Ἄργεος Ἰναχίω.   140
χαῖρε καὶ ἐξελάοισα, καὶ ἐς πάλιν αὖτις ἐλάσσαις
    ἵππως, καὶ Δαναῶν κλᾶρον ἅπαντα σάω.

bath. At that time his very hounds will dine upon what was formerly their master, and his mother will gather her son's bones, journeying to every thicket. She will call you highly favoured and blessed in receiving your son back blind from the hills.

So, my companion, cease your lamentation, for many other honours await him from my hands for your sake. For I shall make him a seer fabled by men to come, indeed far more excellent than any other. He shall know the birds, which are propitious, which fly without significance and those of sinister wing. Many oracles shall he deliver to the Boeotians, many to Kadmos, and later to the mighty sons of Labdakos. Also I shall give him a great staff which shall guide his feet according to their need, and a long span of life. And alone, when he dies, shall he roam among the dead with his faculties preserved, respected by the mighty Marshaller of the Folk.'

So speaking she nodded assent. Whatever Pallas nods assent to is accomplished, for to Athene alone of his daughters did Zeus grant this power, to receive all of her father's prerogatives. No mother, attendants, bore the goddess, but the head of Zeus. The head of Zeus does not sanction falsehood; neither then does his daughter.

Now Athene comes truly. Come receive the goddess, girls, whose care is the task, with praise and prayers and pious cries. Hail goddess, and care for Inachian Argos. Hail also when you drive away, and may you drive your team back again and preserve the whole estate of the Danaans.

CHAPTER ONE

A GLANCE AT THE HYMNS

We owe the preservation of the Hymns to the tidy mind of an early scribe who brought together the Hymns of Homer, Kallimachos, Orpheus (and the Orphic *Argonautica*) and Proklos. It is worth bearing in mind what we would now possess but for this fortunate circumstance. Of the 95 lines of the first Hymn we would have some thirteen complete lines, parts of ten others and tatters of papyrus. But this would be sheer luxury compared with the lot of Hymns 5 and 6. Of the latter we would be able to identify only three lines with confidence from ancient testimonia, with fragmentary relics on papyrus. *Of the former, the subject of this study, we could not place a single line.* Lines are not assigned to the Hymn on the rare occasions on which they are quoted, and—presumably by accident—the Hymn is not represented among the papyri. Among the hymns fewest ancient testimonia survive for Hs. 5 and 6 and, even if Poseidippos (*Anth. Pal.* V. 202.4 ἑσπερινῶν πώλων ἄρτι φρυασσομένων; cf. H. 5.2) does really demonstrate an early regard for the *Bath of Pallas*, beyond an allusion or two in Propertius and Tibullus we have little to show that its merits continued to be recognized. [1]

It is frequently regretted today that the Hymns are the only complete work of the poet to survive (for we have only a selection of his epigrams). This complaint is not difficult to appreciate. The sizable fragments of the *Hecale* and *Aitia* which are now accessible to us give an impression of greater relaxation from the point of view of style and content. But, for good or ill, with all their richness, variety and the obscurity which time, no less than design, has

---

[1] I should perhaps add a mention of Charal Floratos' detection of the influence of H. 5 in Ov. *Fast.* iv. 133-162, a description of the *Veneralia*, involving a bath of Venus' statue. In *Herm.* 88 (1960), 197-216 the author divides Kallimachos' poem into 11 sections, 8 of which he finds represented in Ovid. These divisions seem to me artificial (they cut across the natural ones suggested by ἔξιτε, ἴτε, ἔξιθι), but Ovid may of course have subdivided the poem as he pleased. Floratos does not give a verdict on Kleinknecht's views. He is interesting when he connects Athene's 'change of heart' and Ovid's use of Venus Verticordia (p. 212).

stamped upon them, the Hymns remain the most substantial surviving relics of the poet's work. As I have mentioned, we could have had a great deal less. Let us be grateful for so fortuitous a transmission, and draw from them what illumination we can.

The Hymns are six in number, and there is no shred of evidence to suggest that Kallimachos ever wrote more. Their subjects are I. Zeus 2. Apollo 3. Artemis 4. Delos 5. Athene (*The Bath of Pallas*) and 6. Demeter. At every level their variety becomes painfully obvious. Five of the hymns are written in dactylic hexameters, one, the fifth, in elegiac couplets. Four of the hymns are written in epic-Ionic, but the fifth and sixth in literary Doric. Three (Hs. 1, 2, 4) flatter the Ptolemies. Again three (Hs. 2, 5, 6) plunge us into an atmosphere of excited expectation, the reactions of the faithful awaiting a divine epiphany. Again, the poems differ in purpose. Hymn I, which ends with a prayer for both virtue and wealth, is often construed as the artful dodge of Kallimachos in his early days of poverty to gain recognition from Ptolemy Philadelphos, in the spirit of the American parody: 'Alleluia, give us a handout to revive us again'. H. 2 is assumed, certainly wrongly, to be designed to reconcile Kallimachos' native city, Cyrene, to the overlordship of Egypt. H. 4, a glorification of Delos and built around the story of Leto's search for a land which would have the courage to ignore Hera's hostility and assist at the birth of Apollo, contains a deification of Philadelphos which may be more important than its subordinate position suggests. Hymns 3, 5 and 6 (at least) have a literary purpose.

Again, Hymns 1, 2, 5 and (in a special way) 6 may be separated from the other two by the way in which the poet superimposes images. This point is worth elaborating. If I say more in this chapter about Hymns 1 and 2 than 3 and 4 it is because the former have more significant points of contact with Hs. 5 and 6. Moreover one can extract more from them, even if one cannot lay claim to understanding them. In truth—something about which it pays to be frank—H. 3 is an enigma to me, and also part of the purpose of H. 4. [1] I can take comfort only in the fact that, even in this year of grace and with an author as diligently studied as Vergil, it would be unwise to risk money on behalf of another's claim that he understood the *Eclogues*.

---

[1]   I am reserving for a larger study the solution to H. 2, which has always excited the greatest interest among scholars. In the interest of one specific

It was the Ptolemaic ruler-cult which provided a ready-made opportunity for studies in ambivalence. Where kings and queens became gods and goddesses by royal decree, and enterprising parts of the empire were prepared to pay them such honours during their lifetimes (and Ptolemy Philadelphos was to legitimize the practice), a poet—particularly a court poet—had ample opportunity to garnish the hymnal form with judicious overlapping of images. It is a reflection of Kallimachos' mischievous spirit that he does not sustain the device throughout the first two hymns. I know that there have been scholars with a differing viewpoint, but if this study establishes anything, it draws attention to Kallimachos as 'the mischievous poet', who delights in the ebb and flow of images and challenges us to detect when his semantic tide is on the turn. I trust, also, that the reader will notice in retrospect that it is *a priori* likely that both Hs. 1 and 2 precede Hs. 5 and 6, precisely because the identification of god and ruler calls for no display of the imagination, whereas the nature of the levels of reference in Hs. 5 (taken from popular piety) and 6 (taken from literature) suggests that they are developments of the feature.

The first hymn starts with Zeus. The image is quite clear, for the poet debates whether the god was born in Crete or Arcadia. Arcadia, he says, must win, for Cretans are notorious liars, and they prove this by exhibiting Zeus' grave. But what of lines 57 ff., in

---

question, the Callimachean *sophisma*, I have incorporated at p. 50 a few remarks on the structure of the hymn. When treating H. 2 I shall have more to say about Prof. H. Erbse's study in *Hermes* 83 (1955). He introduces a new theory on the structure of the Epiphany Hymns, that ritual opening and cautionary tale (Hs. 5 and 6) or the more diffuse central stanzas of H. 2 harmonize to present the abstraction of divinity in a form which we can grasp. The epiphany takes place at a point in the poem at which the poet can say: 'Now, by my characterization, I have brought the real Apollo (or Athene or Demeter) before your eyes'. It will be obvious from this present study that we cannot both be right, but, since Erbse is primarily concerned with H. 2, I thought it would be fairer to study the question in a context where some of his ideas can the more easily be given their due. Perhaps the pages which follow will produce the reactions which prompted F. Lasserre (*Rh. Mus.* 102 (1959), 326) to initiate discussion of a problem in Theokritos with the remark: 'Il est difficile aujourd'hui de faire accepter une interprétation allégorique'. I can only say in advance that allegory is at the heart of H. 2 and that the question of the interpretation of H. 2.29, which I use as an illustration on p. 17, becomes the important problem of the poem for the determination of the recipient of the hymn. But the significant contribution to literature is not that H. 2 contains allegory, *but that Hs. 2, 5 and 6 are 'leg-pulls'*.

which Kallimachos quarrels with the commonsense of the orthodox view that Zeus, Poseidon and Pluto drew lots for Heaven, Sea and Earth? Only fools, argues the poet, would draw lots for unequal prizes, for Olympos and Hades. The truth is that Zeus' elder brothers magnanimously recognized his merits as a warrior and installed him in Heaven. This seems to me to involve transparent flattery. 'The suggestion is that the elder son of Ptolemy Soter should have acted similarly, something he had in fact failed to do (Körte, *Hellenistic Poetry*, p. 105; cf. A. Lesky, *Gesch. d. gr. Lit.*, p. 643). The fact that Homer (*Il.* 15. 190 ff.) presents the view of the partition which Kallimachos rejects, and Hesiod (*Theog.* 881) that which the poet accepts, has invited the conclusion that H. 1.57 ff. is simply an exercise in literary polemics. But Kallimachos protests too much; he is a little too anxious to establish his case. After all is not ἐπ' ἰσαίῃ γὰρ ἔοικε πήλασθαι 63-4 ('It is proper to cast lots on equal terms') a piece of special pleading? If Hades is to be thought of as a booby prize, then only a fool would accept it without a chance at a higher prize. When the poet talks of 'equality' he argues from the premise that each party has offered a region *as his stake*; but we should know better.

When Kallimachos flatters Ptolemy as a mighty warrior (66 f.) he follows a course which Theokritos also considered diplomatic (*Id.* 17.56 f., 103). To be sure history tells another story (Gow *ad locc. cit.*), but the conceit was harmless. However reference to the troubled rise of Philadelphos to power was a risky business; Ptolemy might misconstrue his meaning. And so the poet has provided the allusion with a perfectly respectable facade, a suggestion of that new respect for Hesiod which is a characteristic of the age. If Ptolemy takes umbrage Kallimachos is ready with his bearing of injured innocence. [1] Zeus is now Ptolemy Philadelphos and, we may conclude, freshly risen to power. We may notice it as a curiosity— although no part of the poet's plan [2]— that Zeus' brothers may very properly be deemed *philadelphoi*. But Callimachean images are seldom simple; the poet prefers kaleidoscopic variety. And so he retraces his steps. 'From Zeus come kings, since nothing is diviner

---

[1] This seems to me the answer to Herter's charge (*R.E.* Supp. V 437-8) that the context lacks the high seriousness which would be necessary for allusion to such a ticklish subject. A direct and serious approach would make escape difficult even for one endowed (as we shall see) with some of the skills of a Houdini.

[2] See Volkmann, *R.E.* xxiii, 2 (1959), 1645.50 ff.

than the kings of Zeus' (78-9) [1], and most highly blessed of all is 'our ruler' (84-9). That is to say, kings are *diogeneis*, and especially Philadelphos. Is Zeus now Philadelphos' father, Ptolemy Soter? Possibly. At least he is not Philadelphos. But the poet moves forward again.

The *envoi* (91-6) contains a prayer to the divinity for virtue and wealth. From Hom. Hymn 15. 9, 20. 8 and Buck, *Greek Dialects* (1955), p. 227 [2] we gather that it is a traditional formula. But Kallimachos uses repetition in a way which is highly suspicious: 'not wealth without virtue, nor virtue without wealth, but virtue and wealth'. We now have no doubt that the earthly king is uppermost in the poet's thoughts. The distinctive result is that the poem contains two levels of reference, but the pattern is not so thoroughgoing that we can think of simple and consistent allegory. The one image is at one moment elevated, at another subordinated, and consistently within the confines of a formal harmony. This is the principal way in which Kallimachos exploits the hymnal form, by weaving sporadically into his hymn an alien strand, but of similar texture to the general composition. It is a strand which transforms the composition, either announcing the poet's purpose (as here) or,

---

[1] A tantalizingly simple set of words, but it is impossible to get any meaning out of them which does not involve some tautology or other irregularity: ἐπεὶ Διὸς οὐδὲν ἀνάκτων θειότερον. The translation 'Among kings nothing is more divine than Zeus' strains θειότερον, which is better predicated of earthly ἄνακτες than heavenly Zeus. Cf. θεώτερος at H. 2.93 (of the chorus at Cyrene) and 3.249 (of the shrine of Artemis at Ephesos). 'Hesiod hat die Könige auf Zeus zurückgeführt, denn etwas Göttlicheres als die (echten) διογενεῖς βασιλῆες gibt es nicht' (Wilamowitz, *Hell. Dicht.* II 9 f.; cf. Herter, Bursian 255, p. 196) seems to me to involve a circular argument; is, moreover, the double genitive really explained by reference to Hesiod *Op.* 253 (e.g. Herter, *loc. cit.* and Desrousseaux, *R.E.G.* 53 (1940), 157)?

If there is a corruption in the lines it is therefore most likely to be at ἐπεὶ Διός, and emendations have been legion. I hesitantly suggest ἐπ' εἴδεος. 'Kings are from Zeus' is taken from Hes. *Theog.* 96, a passage which is closely related to *Od.* 8.167 ff. (see e.g. F. Solmsen, *T.A.P.A.* 85 (1954), 8-13). In the latter there is some discussion about *eidos* (169, 176, especially 174 ἄλλος δ' αὖ εἶδος μὲν ἀλίγκιος ἀθανάτοισιν). I would translate 'Kings come from Zeus. In regard to (lit. 'in the case of') appearance nothing is more divine than kings'. Ἐπ' εἴδεος . . . θειότερος paraphrases θεοειδής. We may either understand something like σκοποῦντι with ἐπ' εἴδεος (for the idiom see Kühner-Gerth, II i, 497 f.), or take it as an independent usage (exx. of ἐπί and gen. as 'concerning', 'in the case of' in Moulton-Milligan, *The Vocabulary of the Greek Testament*, p. 233 s.v.). H. 4. 114 ἐπ' ἐμεῖο does not seem to me to be markedly different.

[2] Cf. Pindar *Ol.* 2.58, *Pyth.* 5.1 (for other examples from Pindar, Smiley, *Hermathena* 18 (1919), 53); Theocr. 17.137 (and Gow ad loc.).

as in the 'epiphany' hymns (where it constitutes a special device which I have called later, for want of a more inspired name, a *sophisma*), safeguarding the poet, and the reader, from excessive attention to the rich emotional content of that type of composition.

Although an 'epiphany' hymn, H. 2 is a companion piece to H. 1. Both Zeus as king and Apollo as patron of the arts have earthly counterparts. At the opening Apollo is returning from his holidays. Nature falls silent before the paean of welcome; also those who perpetually mourn, Thetis for her Achilles, and metamorphosed Niobe. This leads artistically, *via* the thought that Niobe's grief over her children, slain by Apollo and Artemis, was the result of her boast that she was superior to Leto in fecundity, to the utterance: 'Cry Hié! Hié! It is an ill thing to vie with the Blessed Ones. He who fights with the Blessed would fight with my king; he who fights with my king would fight also with Apollo'. Apollo and king are set side by side, bound together by a mysterious, ill-defined bond which excites our interest: Apollo and Ptolemy are ὁμοφρονέοντες. In lines 97-103 an aition is provided for the ritual cry ἰὴ ἰὴ παιῆον, based on ἵει, ἵει 'shoot, shoot', the cry raised by the Delphians when Apollo joined battle with the dread Python. 'A helper from the first your mother bore you, and ever since that is your praise' (103-4). Kallimachos finishes with an example of Apollo's help:

> 'Envy spoke furtively into the ear of Apollo: "I don't think much of the poet who does not sing the loud song of the sea". [1] Apollo kicked Envy away and retorted: "Mighty is the current of the Euphrates, but it carries on its waters much litter and garbage. And not of every water do her priestesses carry to Demeter, but of the water pure and undefiled that springs up from a hallowed fountain, a trickling stream, the finest flower of water".'

The *envoi*, short and crisp, prays that Blame may join Envy, expelled from the Heavenly circle.

Of course this literary quarrel is not conducted at a celestial level. Envy and Blame stand for definite, although unknown, critics of Kallimachos. We cannot help thinking of the critics pilloried by the poet as the Telchines, malevolent Rhodian spirits, in the preface to his *Aitia*, the more so as in the same passage Apollo

---

[1] οὐκ ἄγαμαι τὸν ἀοιδὸν ὃς οὐδ' ὅσα πόντος ἀείδει. I take ἀείδει as the logical verb for πόντος. Kallimachos is surely thinking of the πολύφλοισβος θάλασσα. We should remember the similar reference at fr. 1. 19-20 (cf. 29-30) μηδ' ἀπ' ἐμεῦ διφᾶτε μέγα ψοφέουσαν ἀοιδὴν τίκτεσθαι· βροντᾶν οὐκ ἐμόν, ἀλλὰ Διός.

presents to the poet his literary manifesto. Hence Apollo assuredly stands for a Ptolemy, Ptolemy the patron, the champion; and, we may suspect, H. 2 is the poet's paean to him. We find ourselves then wondering exactly how much of the poem really is divorced from a retrospective double reference. The sight of Apollo ensures greatness (10). 'We shall see you, Farworker, and we shall never be lowly' (11). Is Ptolemy definitely excluded? The alien strand is so similar in texture to the material of the form that we cannot be sure. There are some who have not been able to identify it at all, as we shall see in Chapters II and V. In a sense, we are all interlopers here. H. 2 is not written for us, no *monumentum aere perennius*; it was all for Ptolemy's benefit. What mattered most was to give his flattered patron opportunity to find his reflection mirrored in the poem at the second reading. Here we may merely note how the poet invites our confusion by a formal respect for the type of composition which he employs. Even Apollo's act in expelling Envy with a kick, which Bethe noted as most ungodlike, is *formally* balanced by line 3; the god who kicks the door in welcome kicks Envy in dismissal. It is the departure in sense from the Homeric hymn which indicates the poet's mischievous intervention.

If then H. 1 is reasonably regarded as an early plea for royal favour and recognition, H. 2 seems a later act of thanksgiving for royal protection. There is a distinctly personal tone to the poem: 'my king' (26-7) . . .'my city' (65) . . . . 'our kings' (68) . . . 'But I call you Karneios; such is the manner of my fathers' (71). As Chamoux [1] observes: 'Le ἐμοὶ πατρώιον οὕτω sonne très haut'. It is particularly unfortunate that our complete understanding of the imagery of H. 2 is crippled by chronological problems. I would gladly bypass them completely, for this is not a suitable moment to ventilate the subject adequately, but at least the choice confronting us must be mentioned. It is generally, but not always, assumed that the hymn is late, an idea which has recently been challenged by Prof. Von der Mühll [2]. An early date suggests Philadelphos again as the human term of reference, while a late date may turn our thoughts to his successor, Ptolemy Euergetes, who became sole ruler in 247. The *Lock of Berenice* establishes that the poet was still productive after this date, but, according to the theory, H. 2 could have been written before the death of Philadelphos.

---

[1] *Cyrène sous la monarchie des Battiades*, p. 303 n. 1.
[2] *Mus. Helv.* 15 (1958), 1-10.

The scholiast at line 26 took 'my king' to refer to Euergetes, διὰ δὲ τὸ φιλόλογον αὐτὸν εἶναι ὡς θεὸν τιμᾷ. Perhaps this is no more than a guess, and may be based on the line which gives the identification most point: δύναται γάρ, ἐπεὶ Διὶ δεξιὸς ἧσται (29). Now a reference to the source of the divinity's power is traditional, and Kallimachos plays upon this fact again at H. 5. 131 ff. We may compare Pindar fr. 146 Snell, where Athene sits on the right hand of Zeus and receives his commandments for the gods. The problem is the question of whether both Zeus and Apollo are allegorical terms at this point, or whether only Apollo has an earthly counterpart. If the former, we recall that in H. 1 Zeus and Philadelphos are identified. The poet would hark back to his earlier hymn. In fact the equation of Zeus and Philadelphos is almost canonical. For example, at Theocr. *Id.* 7. 93 Simichidas, representing Theokritos in his youth, says that he would not be surprised if his poems had already been brought by report to 'the throne of Zeus'. [1] Meleager (*Anth. Pal.* VII. 418. 3) talks of 'Kos which reared Zeus', for Philadelphos was born on that island. Theokritos (*Id.* 17. 131) compares Philadelphos' married life with his sister Arsinoe to the *hieros gamos* of Zeus and Hera. We would then have to seek in Apollo a co-regent of Philadelphos.

Now we do hear of a co-regent from 267/6, but he is always 'Ptolemy the son'. Since the title Euergetes was not assumed until between the third and fifth year of his reign, it was once supposed that 'Ptolemy the son' is Euergetes. To this identification, in the present state of our knowledge, Volkmann, who has recently studied the evidence in *R.E.* xxiii, 2 (1959), 1666. 26 ff. and 1668. 35 ff., has raised serious objections. Again, Apollo as Euergetes seems to give special significance to the poet's historical sketch of the foundation of Cyrene under Apollo's guidance, for Euergetes was betrothed to Berenice, the daughter of Magas, king of Cyrene. But Kallimachos had valid reasons for discussing Cyrene since it was his native city. Moreover that this episode is so important that the opening epiphany scene is to be localised in Cyrene is a quite unnecessary assumption. And yet Apollo may still be Euergetes, promoted to a partnership, which he did not formally enjoy, by a grateful poet. Such a liberty would fall short of being outrageous, for Philadelphos, as Zeus, would not be deprived of his meed of honour.

[1] See B. A. van Groningen, *Mnem.* S. IV. 2 (1959), 42-3.

The alternative is to assume Apollo to be Philadelphos the patron, the counterpart of Zeus as Philadelphos the king in H. 1. Here again we meet a choice. Is Zeus then his father, Ptolemy Soter, who had been deified along with his wife as the 'Saviour Gods'? Hardly likely, when Philadelphos' co-regency was as early as 285-283 and the tense of ἧσται demands a present reality; but Soter may now be Zeus Soter, enthroned in Heaven. Or is Zeus simply his celestial self? Philadelphos then becomes Zeus' most honoured son, just as at one stage in H. 1 this king is the divinest of kings, honoured by Zeus. If we could be confident of this identi-fication, we might find it of a little use for chronological purposes. In H. 1 the image fluctuates between Zeus, Ptolemy=Zeus and *Ptolemy* who derives his power from Zeus, in H. 2 between Apollo, Ptolemy=Apollo and *Apollo=Ptolemy* who derives his power from Zeus. That is to say, there would be a development in the imagery. At this stage in the first hymn Ptolemy is 'divinest of the kings of Zeus', while in the second he is unequivocally a god. This would suggest that H. 1 precedes, while H. 2 follows, Phila-delphos' open assumption of divine honours (c. 271/0 B.C.).

Much more could be said, but it would serve no purpose. Better to practice angelic, even archangelic, caution, for the elucidation of Kallimachos from Ptolemaic chronology is the explanation of the obscure *per obscurius*. And yet, whether Philadelphos or Euergetes is involved, the fact of the double level of reference stands firm.

We have examined at some length the interaction of dominant images in the first two hymns because Hymns 5 and 6 also feature a similar play. But the technique is also used at a lower level. For example, at H. 4. 47-9 Delos, when a wandering island under the name of Asterie, swam to the 'water-drenched *maston* of the island Parthenie (for it was not yet Samos)'. Μαστός is at the same time 'breast' and 'hill'. As Prof. C. del Grande (*Filologia Minore*, p. 244) reminds us, a double image is possible because of the poetic conceit that an island is a giant nymph lying in the sea. Particularly one with so feminine a name as Parthenie. The device had already been noted as Pindaric by G. Norwood (*Pindar*, pp. 35, 38) and J. Duchemin (*Pindare*, pp. 141-2). Pindar liked to blend the images of a city and its eponymous nymph, as at *Pyth.* 4. 8, where Battos is sent to found Cyrene ἐν ἀργινόεντι μαστῷ. It is interesting to find him applying the same technique to Delos, and then in an unequi-vocal form (*Paean* 5. 39-42):

ἐρικυδέα τ' ἔσχον
Δᾶλον, ἐπεί σφιν 'Απόλλων
δῶκεν ὁ χρυσοκόμας
'Αστερίας δέμας οἰκεῖν.

We may justly say of Kallimachos what H. Fränkel (*Ovid*, p. 99) found good reason to say of Ovid's interest in metamorphosis: 'The theme gave ample scope for displaying the phenomena of insecure and fleeting identity, of a self divided in itself or spilling over into another self'.

The Hellenistic circle had a special regard for the ambivalent in language, or what could pass for ambivalence, for this, after all, is the stuff of metaphor. When we find in Kallimachos a rare word, we shall learn nothing if we merely catalogue the use as recherché, and close our minds to the factors which prompt the use. When words cease to be affective they often cease to be effective for the poet. He finds himself obliged to reestablish the imagery, perhaps in a different direction, or to restore lost sonority, perhaps on the basis of principles of which an earlier age was not conscious. He had above all to overcome the handicap of a lingua franca, the *Koine*, which gave little encouragement to poetic endeavour. The rare word, then, may convey a desirable sound or may add a new dimension to the imagery. The common word may equally be renovated by changing its associations or by recalling it to an etymology which it had by lapse of time outgrown. In Kallimachos it pays to be sensitive to both new and old, for we have the added complicating factors of the degree of conformity of the language to a particular type of composition (e.g. the language of the *Epigrams* and H. 5 is rather different from that of the *Aitia*), and of the strong possibility of pointed literary reference. Again and again we are driven back to our lexica to find the antecedents of a usage; the results are so rewarding that we can only regret the more keenly the passing of so much literature which must have been exposed to the poet's excerpting passion.

In H. 5 there is not a good deal in the way of special verbal effects. The language is refined because too many distractions will put Kallimachos' purpose beyond our recall. But there are some effects. For example, at lines 75-6. There could not have been a poet of any standing who had not had occasion more than once to describe the bloom of youth; the subject must have been a continual challenge to a clever poet. Kallimachos swings into the image in the hexameter with ἄρτι γένεια, and when the pentameter opens we are surprised to find περκάζων as the verb, for it is appropriate to ripening grapes. In fact he is appropriating, with characteristic modification, an image from Euripides' *Cretans* [1]: σέλας οἰνωπὸν ἐξέλαμπε περκαίνων γένυν (of Pasiphae's bull!). One of a quieter kind occurs in line 12, where the horses' mouths are χαλινοφάγοι. He might have said χαλινοδάκοι (cf. στό-μιον δάκνειν, Aesch. *P.V.* 1009, τὸν χαλινὸν ἐνδακεῖν Pl. *Phdr.* 254 d), but the frothing of the horses' mouths suggested mastication, not mere biting. English has the same transfer in 'to champ the bit', for which verb the Oxford English Dictionary defines the primary meaning as 'munch (fodder) noisily'. Latin is no diffe-rent with its *mandere*, e.g. Verg. *Aen.* 4. 135: stat sonipes ac frena ferox spumantia mandit.

There are clearer examples in H. 6. At lines 94-5 we are told: 'His mother wailed, and his two sisters lamented bitterly, and the breast that he used to drink and the many tens of handmaids'. 'The breast that he used to drink' is of course Erysichthon's wet-nurse, but it is more than a simple case of *synecdoche*, the part for the whole. The logical verb for 'breast' in the sentence is 'lamented' (ἔστενε . . . . μαστός). We then begin to remember that beating the breast was a regular way for women to express grief, and that Kallimachos is again playing upon two levels of reference. Again at line 105. Through the insatiable hunger of Erysichthon the food supply of the palace is rapidly being exhausted. 'The cattle stalls are empty', but the adjective used by the poet is χῆραι, 'widowed'. The idea of 'bereavement' adds a pathetic overtone to Triopas' plea to Poseidon. Lastly we shall notice one not so success-ful. Erysichthon's parents try to conceal their disgrace, but this is impossible ὅκα τὸν βαθὺν οἶκον ἀνεξήραναν ὀδόντες (113). The house is βαθύς, 'prosperous', 'wealthy'. Kallimachos associates this meta-phorical idea of 'depth' with a pit or well, hence the forceful ἀνε-ξήραναν, 'they dried up the (deep)house'. This is bearable, but the subject is 'his teeth', which must then be thought of as a searing wind drying up even a deep well. This is venturesome, to say the

---

[1] Fr. 15; Page, *Greek Literary Papyri* (Loeb) I p. 74. A great number of the poet's semantic shifts are collected by C. del Grande, *Filologia Minore* (Milan-Naples 1956), Ch. 23. I am not always in agreement with him on his explanations, but his examples are generally sound.

least, but perhaps we should bear in mind that the Erysichthon tale is burlesque, and humorous exaggeration must consequently enjoy some concession.

We shall also find it useful to consider some of the elements which make the amalgam of a Callimachean hymn. At the summit Homer reigns, but precisely because he is a colossus of unique power no Hellenist sought merely to be stamped as *Homerikotatos*. While many Hellenistic scholars are known to have been keen commentators on the Homeric texts, both those who approved of an epic canvass of its original dimensions and those who did not strove to innovate. It was customary to modify when borrowing, as at H. 5. 104, where the thought of *Il.* 20. 127-8 (Αἶσα | γιγνομένῳ ἐπένησε λίνῳ, ὅτε μιν τέκε μήτηρ) and *Il.* 24. 209-210 (Μοῖρα κραταιὴ | γιγνομένῳ ἐπένησε λίνῳ, ὅτε μιν τέκον αὐτή) appears in the form: ἐπεὶ Μοιρᾶν ὧδ᾽ ἐπένησε λίνα, | ἁνίκα τὸ πρᾶτόν νιν ἐγείναο. The most surprising thing is the rise of Hesiod; not simply as a more approachable standard, but for positive reasons. He was to them a polymath with wide interests, a didactic poet who paid careful attention to sound, and, as the supposed author of the *Catalogue of Women*, a mythological mine, a model for narrative art, with even a curious reputation for love poetry.

But far more important was the Hellenistic eagerness to give new life to limp traditional forms by blending the Classical genres. Kallimachos' formal model, the Homeric Hymn, was heavily indebted to the epic and, generally speaking, breathed the atmosphere of an earlier age of piety. It does not do to overstate the latter point. They are not religious outpourings, and the Hymn to Hermes, for example, is as modern in its playfulness as a Callimachean production. The deep dependence on Homer, which strengthened the tradition that Homer was their author, at any rate stamped them collectively as archaic. The most obvious importation into Kallimachos' hymns is a pronounced lyrical flavour. [1] We need not think of it as a preserve of our poet. I think particularly of an attractive fragment of a kind of *partheneion* to Demeter, in a mixture of Aeolic and Doric, almost certainly of the Hellenistic period. [2]

---

[1] See Cahen, *Callimaque*, pp. 310 ff., for a full discussion.

[2] *P. Oxy.* I 8; *Collectanea Alexandrina*, p. 186 Powell. Cahen, *Callimaque*, p. 315, and others think that it shows Callimachean influence. I am not convinced that there is any real evidence for the tendency to find the in-

"Ηνθομεν ἐς μεγάλας Δαμάτερος ἐννέ' ἐάσσαι,
παῖσαι παρθενικαί, παῖσαι καλὰ ἔμματ' ἔχοισαι,
καλὰ μὲν ἔμματ' ἔχοισαι, ἀριπρεπέας δὲ καὶ ὅρμως
πριστῶ ἐξ ἐλέφαντος, ἰδῆν ποτεοικότας . . . .

'We are nine young maids who went to Church, all wearing our
Sunday best'. It is hard not to think of Gilbert and Sullivan.

A lyrical element in the hymnal form reminds us that lyricists
also wrote hymns. Apart from Pindar, whose influence is almost
omnipresent, [1] it is only seldom that we have the means to gauge
the extent of their influence upon Kallimachos; but what we find
suggests that it was strong. For example, H. 3 opens with forty
lines of discussion between a wheedling three-year-old Artemis and
her indulgent father, 'das Baby Artemis auf Papa Zeus' Schoss', [2]
in which the goddess prattles about the presents she would like,
and finds a responsive ear. A few lines of Lesbian poetry, attributed
without certainty to Alkaios, provided the inspiration:

> I vow that I shall ever be virgin, a huntress on the peaks of lonely
> mountains. Come, grant these favours for my sake." So she spoke; and the
> father of the blessed gods nodded assent.' [3]

More important for us, because of the epiphany motif, is Alkaios'
Hymn to Apollo, of which only the first line survives. Fortunately
the contents are summarized for us by Himerius (Or. xiv. 10 f. =
xlviii. 10 f. Colonna). Apollo, sent by Zeus to Delphi to speak as
prophet of justice and right to Hellas, disobediently spends a
year among the Hyperboreans. The Delphians compose a paean and
beseech the god to come back. Eventually he does.

> 'Now it was summer, and indeed midsummer, when Alkaios brings
> Apollo back from the Hyperboreans. And so, because the summer was

fluence of H. 6 behind the various Hellenistic hymns, or other types of
composition, addressed to Demeter. For example, an anonymous hymn to
Demeter of the 3rd. c. B.C. (Page, Gk. Lit. Pap. no. 91) has the Homeric
account of the allocation by lot of Heaven, Earth and Hell. To Roberts
(Aegyptus, 14 (1934), 447)—with Page's approval—the author is contrad-
icting Kallimachos' H. 1. Surely this does not follow. Still less the idea that
Page, Gk. Lit. Pap. no. 122 is indebted to Kallimachos' H. 6, when the only
point of contact is the use of βούβρωστις, and then not necessarily with the
same meaning.

[1] See M. T. Smiley, Hermathena 18 (1919), 46-69.
[2] Bethe's attractive phrase (Gr. Dichtung, p. 305).
[3] Alc. T 1, lines 3-8 Lobel-Page, with Page's supplements in Sappho and
Alcaeus, pp. 261 ff. (see page 264 for Kallimachos).

aglow, and Apollo was at home (ἐπιδημοῦντος Ἀπόλλωνος), even the lyre puts on a summer-dress, so to speak, in honour of the god (θερινόν τι καὶ ἡ λύρα περὶ τὸν θεὸν ἀβρύνεται). The nightingales sing him the kind of song you expect of birds in Alkaios; swallows and cicadas sing, forgetting to tell of their own sufferings among men, and devoting their songs wholly to the god. Kastalia flows, in poetic vein, with streams of silver, and the waves of Kephisos heave and surge, like Homer's Enipeus. For Alkaios, like Homer, perforce makes even the water capable of perceiving the gods' presence (θεῶν ἐπιδημίαν).' [1]

The interest which this has for Kallimachos' H. 2. 1-24 becomes obvious.

'How the laurel sapling of Apollo trembles! How the whole shrine trembles! Away, away, he that is sinful! Now surely Phoibos is striking the door with his lovely foot. Don't you see? The Delian palm nods merrily all at once, and the swan sings sweetly in the air! Now of yourselves swing back, you bars of the gates, swing back of yourselves, you bolts! For the god is no longer distant. And do you, young lads, prepare yourselves for song and dance.

Not to every man does Apollo appear, but to him who is good. He who sees him, he is great; who sees him not is of low estate. We shall see you, Farworker, and we shall never be lowly. The lads are not to keep lyre silent or tread noiseless when Apollo is at home (Φοίβου ἐπιδημήσαντος), if they wish to accomplish marriage and cut hoary locks, and the wall to stand upon its ancient foundations. Well done, lads! For the lyre is no longer idle. Be hushed as you hear the song to Apollo. Hushed even the sea, when singers glorify the lyre or bow, the weapons of Lycorean Apollo. Not even Thetis wails a mother's lament for Achilles, when she hears the cry 'Hié Paiéon! Hié Paiéon!' And the tearful rock defers its grief, the wet stone that is set in Phrygia, a marble rock in the stead of a woman, uttering sorrowful words from an open mouth.'

Both hymns concern an *epidemia* of Apollo, and in both the excitement runs high. What is particularly interesting is the complete diversity of illustration within common themes. There is the same excited reaction of Apollo's impersonal associates, but in Alkaios it is his lyre (given to him at his birth, whence he invented lyre playing, Alc. α 1 (b) Lobel-Page—perhaps from this same hymn), in Kallimachos the sacred laurel, palm and the whole of the shrine. In both birds also react. Alkaios features the nightingales, Kallimachos the swans. (In Alkaios Apollo has a chariot of swans.) Gloom is dispelled in both versions. In Alkaios the swallows and cicadas forget their sufferings (immortalized in the Prokne-Philomela and Tithonos stories); in Kallimachos it is Thetis and Niobe. We notice, incidentally, that the former react to the presence of Apollo, the latter to the paean itself. In both versions water

---

[1] Cf. also Bowra, *Greek Lyric Poetry*, pp. 171 ff.; Page, *op. cit.*, pp. 244 ff.

reacts. In the earlier Kephisos heaves and surges with joy, in the latter the sea is reverently hushed. When Alkaios' Kastalia flows with streams of silver, there is probably the same honorific intention that we find in H. 5. 49 ff., where Inachos brings down gold and blossoms on its waters, and in Moschos 3. 1-3, where Alpheus courts Arethusa, his waters bearing beautiful leaves and blossoms and holy dust from the race-course at Olympia.

Such unity in diversity admits of only two explanations: either Kallimachos is completely remodelling Alkaios, or there is a specialized lyric hymn centring upon the *epidemia* of Apollo, either inaugurated by Alkaios or a common possession of both poets. In either case, the parallel invites the conclusion that H. 2 is earlier than Hs. 5 and 6. These three hymns feature an arresting dramatic-mimetic opening to an epiphany. Hs. 5 and 6, we shall see, are closely connected and highly specialised compositions. Hymn 2 stands apart from both in dialect, and from H. 5 in metre. Either H. 2 precedes, or follows, Hs. 5 and 6. The clue is, I think, given by the fact that in the last two hymns the epiphany is incidental to the poet's purpose. He does not say to himself 'I shall construct an epiphany hymn'. He says instead 'I shall do something with this story of Teiresias' (H. 5) and 'I shall do something more with this Doric dialect' (H. 6). If the rest of this study has any merit, in Hs. 5 and 6 Kallimachos is using the epiphany motif as something already found satisfying and successful. And it was earlier found successful in a composition which borrowed the excitement of an epiphany from a lyric hymn. In other words, since we know of a hymn by Alkaios featuring an epiphany of Apollo, it is *a priori* likely that Kallimachos developed the idea first in his Hymn to Apollo, for which the basic idea came readymade, and then maintained the technique in Hs. 5 and 6. At the same time (a matter of intuition, I fear), I would not be inclined to put H. 2 *much* earlier than the later pair.

In the face of the variety which I have been illustrating, it is unlikely that we shall ever find a master-key to unlock the door of every hymn. Certainly every attempt hitherto has failed. Cahen (*Callimaque*, pp. 247 ff.) disposes of them all—that they were written by royal command, were allegorical glorifications of the Ptolemies, were liturgical poems, were poems written for poetic contests held during religious festivals. Cahen's own theory is equally involved in their fall. He believed that the hymns have a basis in 'une espèce d'ἐπίδειξις, de lecture solennelle, en rapport direct avec la fête religieuse, en dehors pourtant de son programme' (*Callimaque*, pp. 281 f.). He does not help his idea by wedding it to the belief that each poem was declaimed at the very places where the festival was celebrated, and that therefore the poems were directed to a genuine public—but not the *profanum uulgus*, rather 'un public de dévots, capable d'émotion religieuse et d'émotion littéraire aussi'. Whether such an audience could be expected will be implicitly involved in the study of the emotional content of the poems in Chapter V. Kallimachos would have been appalled (or, perhaps more characteristically, entertained) by the prospect. We may at the present day feel confident that Kallimachos wrote in Alexandria for his friends (including some in the highest places), and for them alone; but for the answers to more particular questions we must weigh each poem individually. Let us look, then, at the *Bath of Pallas*.

CHAPTER TWO

HYMN 5: THE GROUNDPLAN

Kallimachos specifically tells us that his 'cautionary' tale is not of his own invention: μῦθος δ' οὐκ ἐμός, ἀλλ' ἑτέρων, 56. It is, after all, dramatically speaking, desirable for the narrator to be able to remove any suspicion that such an edifying stimulus to devotion is home-made. Unfortunately we know it at an earlier date associated only with the name of Pherekydes, and then only through the lacunose texts of pseudo-Apollodoros (*Bibl.* III. vi. 7) and the Townleian scholiast (Hom. *Od.* 10, 493). [1] The former mentions three versions which accounted for Teiresias' blindness—the tale that he was blinded by the gods for revealing their secrets to men, the Hesiodic story (to which we shall return later) and the Phere-cydean version. According to this last Teiresias, the son of Everes and a nymph Chariklo, was blinded by Athene. [2] 'For Chariklo, a close friend of Athene ... (lacuna) .. he saw the goddess stark naked, and covering his eyes with her hands she blinded him. Chariklo begged her to restore his sight, but this the goddess could not do; instead she cleansed his ears to make him understand every birdcall and gave him the gift of a cornel wood staff, by carrying which he walked as well as those with sight.'

The scholiast [3] starts his account with 'Pherekydes says that Teiresias was blinded after he saw Athene bathing in the ...' and when the text resumes we have left the version of Pherekydes and have joined that of Hesiod. For the present we need notice only that there was in fact a version according to which Teiresias

---

[1]   3 F 92 a) and b) Jacoby.

[2]   .. Φερεκύδης δὲ ὑπὸ 'Αθηνᾶς αὐτὸν τυφλωθῆναι· οὖσαν γὰρ τὴν Χαρικλὼ προσφιλῆ τῇ 'Αθηνᾷ <. . . .> γυμνὴν ἐπὶ πάντα ἰδεῖν, τὴν δὲ ταῖς χερσὶ τοὺς ὀφθαλ-μοὺς αὐτοῦ καταλαβομένην πηρὸν ποιῆσαι, Χαρικλοῦς δὲ δεομένης ἀποκαταστῆσαι πάλιν τὰς ὁράσεις, μὴ δυναμένην τοῦτο ποιῆσαι, τὰς ἀκοὰς διακαθάρασαν πᾶσαν ὀρνίθων φωνὴν ποιῆσαι συνεῖναι, καὶ σκῆπτρον αὐτῷ δωρήσασθαι κράνειον, ὃ φέρων ὁμοίως τοῖς βλέπουσιν ἐβάδιζεν.

[3]   Θηβαίου Τειρεσίαο μάντηος ἀλαοῦ]πηρωθῆναι δ' αὐτόν <φησι> Φερεκύδης ἰδόντα τὴν 'Αθηνᾶν λουομένην ἐν τῷ <. . . . .> παρθένον ὑπάρχουσαν καὶ κορευθεῖσαν ὑπ' 'Απόλλωνος εἰς το <. . . .> (ἐν τῷ Van der Valk) καίεσθαι μέλλειν ὑπὸ Εὐήρου τοῦ πατρὸς <. . . . .> εἰς ἄνδρα μεταβαλέσθαι γνώμῃ τοῦ θεοῦ καὶ μίαν τὴν <. . . . .> γενέσθαι. The argument between Zeus and Hera follows.

was blinded by Athene when he surprised the goddess at her bath.

Into the middle of his own account of Teiresias' offence Kallimachos introduces a treatment of the Aktaion story, comfortable words spoken by Athene, to show Chariklo that her suffering could in fact have been much greater. In the future Aktaion would commit an identical offence, have even closer ties with the goddess concerned, namely Artemis, but would be torn to pieces by his dogs. Autonoe, his mother, would search every thicket for his bones. Again we must defer detailed discussion, but it is at this point in the poem that the reader who is attuned to the poet's techniques is invited to ask the question which is so readily associated with the author of the *Aitia*: 'Why?' Why does Artemis punish the offender through his hounds? Obviously because Artemis is a huntress. Then if Athene ignores the opportunity for punishment provided by the presence of Teiresias' dogs (ἁμᾶ κυσὶν, 75), because it does not reflect her nature, why does she punish him through his eyes? When we answer this question we have advanced a considerable way towards understanding the *Bath of Pallas*.

The answer draws us back to the ritual framework. 'On an appointed day', the scholiast informs us, 'the Argive women were accustomed to take the image of Athene *and the shield of Diomedes* and bring them to the river Inachos and wash them there; and this was called the Bath of Pallas'. [1] The scholion in its transmitted form is unsatisfactory, the italicized section being represented by καὶ Διομήδους, which could only mean 'the image of Athene *and Diomedes*'. Meineke in his edition of Kallimachos (1861, p. 78) emended to καὶ τὸ Διομήδους σάκος. In view of the preceding sigma and following *kai*, *sakos* could easily disappear. In any case, there is no doubt that the shield was involved in the annual ceremony, for the poet is quite explicit on this point at lines 35 ff.

Now the image of Athene was believed to be the Palladion, the xoanon of the goddess who occupied the citadel of Troy and was readily identified with Athene, the divinity of the Mycenean stronghold. It was in a real sense a fetish upon which the existence of Troy depended [2]. Hence its abduction by Odysseus and Diomedes

---

[1] ῎Εν τινι ἡμέρᾳ ὡρισμένῃ ἔθος εἶχον αἱ ᾿Αργεῖαι γυναῖκες λαμβάνειν τὸ ἄγαλμα τῆς ᾿Αθηνᾶς καὶ Διομήδους καὶ ἄγειν ἐπὶ τὸν ῎Ιναχον ποταμὸν κἀκεῖσε ἀπολούειν· ὃ δὴ καὶ λουτρὰ ὠνομάζετο τῆς Παλλάδος.

[2] See Nilsson, *Griechische Feste*, p. 86. For a summary of the Palladion myths Grimal, *Dictionnaire de la mythologie grecque et romaine* s.v. is useful.

to bring about the fall of Ilion. But its ancient power clung to it still, and many states laid claim to the possession of the real Palladion, fabricating myths to explain how the genuine article strayed from the hands of Diomedes. The Argives were equally sure that Diomedes had brought it back to Argos.

We are not specifically told in which of the three temples of Athene in Argos the Palladion was housed, but the situation at Troy and the evidence from coinage [1] suggest that it was in the temple of Athene Akria on the citadel or Larisa. The divinity of this temple is also named Athene Polias, 'the guardian of the city', in a sixth century inscription [2]. Two voices have been raised powerfully in protest against this home for the Palladion, those of Wilamowitz (*Hell. Dicht.* II, 14 n. 1) and Kleinknecht (p. 311 n. 2) [3]. They decide in favour of a temple of Athene Oxyderkes which Pausanias (2. 24. 2) places near the temple of Apollo Deiradiotes, but their viewpoints are quite different. Wilamowitz supports this idea because the Palladion and Shield of Diomedes are united in the ritual bath of Pallas, Kleinknecht because to him Palladion and Shield of Diomedes are one and the same. But I am moving too quickly. We must return to Athene Oxyderkes.

ATHENE OXYDERKES

Pausanias records that the temple of this divinity was dedicated by Diomedes, Athene's favourite, in return for a service done to him by the goddess while he was fighting at Troy. The incident occurs at *Iliad* 5. 127 ff., where Athene heeds Diomedes' prayer in battle and declares: 'And I have taken the mist from your eyes which formerly lay upon them, so that you may distinguish clearly both god and man'. Thereby Diomedes was saved from future embarrassment in finding himself unwittingly pitted against invincible and irascible divinities. *According to tradition Diomedes' shield was preserved in this temple.*

Let us look firstly at the cult title. Oxyderkes [4] aroused Wila-

---

[1]   L. Ziehen, *R.E.* xviii, 3 col. 175. Cf. Vollgraff, *Mnem.* 57 (1929), 218.

[2]   *Mnem.* 57 (1929), 208 ff., esp. 217 ff.

[3]   Cahen (*Comm.*, p. 217) also settles for this temple, but does not give his reasons. Vollgraff had earlier subscribed to this view, but rejected it in *Bull. de l'Acad. R. de Belgique, Cl. des lettres*, 1938, p. 39, 4.

[4]   Oxyderkes rather than Oxyderko. See Zwicker (s.v. Oxyderko) and Kruse (s.v. Oxyderkes), *R.E.* xviii, 2 col. 2023.

mowitz' suspicions [1], but not rightly so. It recurs in an inscription of Epidauros (*I.G.* IV 1². 491): 'Οξυδέρκας Διονύσιος πυροφορήσας, where we may surmise, as it generally is surmised, that Athene is again the goddess concerned [2]. Moreover the 'eye motif' recurs in Sparta, where was a temple of Athene Optilitis or Ophthalmitis [3]. Tradition asserted that it was dedicated by Lykurgos in gratitude for the preservation of one of his eyes on this site, after the other had been knocked out by Alkandros, who took exception to Lykurgos' laws. In the case of both Ath. Oxyderkes and Ath. Optilitis it is reasonable to imagine that the cult is older than the tradition, which merely provides an *ad hoc* explanation. But in the case of Oxyderkes it is the explanation which interests us.

The primary meaning of *oxyderkes* is 'sharpsighted'. The adjective is as old as Herodotos (2. 68), the corresponding noun (in the Ionic form ὀξυδερκείη) as old as Demokritos (fr. 119). The idea is as old as Homer: ὀξύτατον δέρκεσθαι, *Il.* 17. 675, 23. 477. But in the *medical* writers it developed a secondary causative meaning 'producing sharpness of sight' [4]. It is this latter meaning which has aligned Athene Oxyderkes with the clarification of Diomedes' eyesight. There is striking confirmation of this in Lucian (*Charon* 7). Charon, from his seat on Mt. Parnassos, admits that he cannot focus his eyesight clearly on the cities beneath his gaze. Hermes, his guide, replies: Ἔχ' ἀτρέμας· καὶ τοῦτο γὰρ ἰάσομαί σοι καὶ ὀξυδερκέστατον ἐν βραχεῖ <σε> ἀποφανῶ παρ' Ὁμήρου τινὰ καὶ πρὸς τοῦτο ἐπῴδην λαβών, κἀπειδὰν εἴπω τὰ ἔπη, μέμνησο μηκέτι ἀμβλυώττειν, ἀλλὰ σαφῶς πάντα ὁρᾶν.

The charm which he employs is our passage from the *Iliad*:

'Αχλὺν δ' αὖ τοι ἀπ' ὀφθαλμῶν ἕλον, ἣ πρὶν ἐπῆεν,
ὄφρ' εὖ γιγνώσκῃς ἡμὲν θεὸν ἠδὲ καὶ ἄνδρα.

Kleinknecht (pp. 311-312) refused to share Wilamowitz' distrust, for he perceived something of the eye motif which dominates the poem. But it is unfortunate that one who could write of 'the connexions of our hymn with the figure of Athene Oxyderko which have hitherto been disregarded' (p. 311 n. 2) did not follow the idea

---

[1] *Hell. Dicht.* II, p. 14 n. 1.
[2] Vollgraff, *Le Sanctuaire d'Apollon pythéen à Argos* (1956), 55 ff., finds evidence which suggests that the cult spread from Epidauros to Argos.
[3] Paus. 3.18.2; Plut. *Lycurg.* 11.
[4] Liddell-Scott-Jones list Diocl. fr. 128; Dsc. 5.5; Gal. 12.263.

through to the end. Of course, to say that Athene Oxyderkes has left any mark on the poem is to require that the association of the cult title with Diomedes' improved vision was already current in Hellenistic times. When we note the number of occasions and ways in which the poet plays upon an eye motif, above all the fact that the divinity who destroys Teiresias' eyesight *improves* it by granting him inner vision, I hope it will be conceded that the illumination thrown upon the structure of the poem by the image is worth the small step into the dark.

It is interesting to notice how ideal was the environment of the cult for the poet's purpose. There was a tradition that the genuine Palladion could be recognized *hastae oculorumque mobilitate* [1]. We seem to know of this belief only through Roman sources, but it could very well derive from Greek. It seems, in either case, undesirable that we should entertain Robert's view (supported by W. R. Halliday) [2], that this is the explanation of Athene's title *Oxyderkes*. That the tradition is Greek is suggested by the similarity of the belief that, in horror at the outrage of Kassandra at the hands of Locrian Ajax in Athene's temple, the Palladion turned its eyes to the roof of the shrine [3]. Eyes, then, have their place in the mythology of the Palladion. Furthermore, the temple which housed the Trojan Palladion at Argos is, as has been mentioned, most probably the temple on the Larisa. This temple we know to have also housed the enigmatic statue of Three-eyed Zeus, the paternal god of Priam and perhaps to be identified with Zeus Herkeios [4]. And, if Kallimachos' fancy ever strayed, he might remember that Argos is a name which has strong associations with multiple vision, πυκνοῖς ὄσσοις δεδορκώς (Aesch. *P.V.* 678-9) [5].

---

[1] Serv. ad Verg. *Aen.* 2. 166; cf. *Aen.* 2. 172, 175.

[2] *The Greek Questions of Plutarch* (1928), p. 193.

[3] Schol. *Il.* 13. 66; (Apollodor.) *Epit.* v. 22; Quint. Smyrn. 13. 420 ff.

[4] Paus. 2. 24, 3; Schol. Eur. *Troad.* 16; T. P. Howe, *A.J.A.* 59 (1955), 287-301.

[5] While strictly *nihil ad rem*, it is worth recalling that Kallimachos' delight in topicalities even extended to a learned interest in optics. It has been known since H. Oppermann's article in *Herm.* 60 (1925), 14-32 that when Kallimachos describes the eye of the Cyclopes as σάκει ἴσα τετραβοείῳ (H. 3. 53), he is utilizing the discovery of Herophilos that the eyeball is enclosed by four membranes. I suspect that Apollonios of Rhodes shows at least an etymological interest in eyes at Arg. III. 92-4, where the text reads: ὑμείων γὰρ ἀναιδήτῳ περ ἐόντι | τυτθή γ' αἰδὼς ἔσσετ' ἐν ὄμμασιν· αὐτὰρ ἐμεῖο | οὐκ ὄθεται. There is reason to believe that Kallimachos always used the Aeolic form ὄθμα for ὄμμα (v. Pfeiffer ad fr. 1. 37); if Apollonios used it here there

It is wretched that we know so little of the cult of Athene Oxyderkes. Even the exact location of the temple is still a matter of
dispute. W. Vollgraff, in his belated publication of the fruits of the
Netherlands excavation in 1902-6 [1], placed the temple on the N.E.
corner of the Aspis, the second acropolis of Argos (over which
towers the Larisa), and next to the temple of Apollo Deiradiotes,
as Pausanias had reported. The identification seems to him established by several representations of the goddess in warlike attire
which were found in the vicinity. But G. Roux [2] believes that
Vollgraff should have returned to an earlier idea of his, that the
tholos was associated with Athene Oxyderkes.

> 'Observons enfin, si l'on peut accorder quelque importance à ce détail,
> que des quatre terrasses de l'Aspis la terrasse de la tholos est celle qui
> découvre la vue la plus vaste sur Argos et sur la plaine argienne, et ceci
> était encore plus vrai au temps où le haut bastion élevait le spectateur de
> plusieurs mètres au-dessus du sol actuel. La déesse à la vue perçante avait
> ainsi sous les yeux la ville et la campagne fertile qu'elle avait pour mission
> de protéger.'

Into such a controversy I cannot enter. But I am interested in
Roux' suggestion that Athene's sharpsightedness is functional.
I find myself wondering (although it is in no way essential for
my argument) whether Athene Oxyderkes was in fact an Athene
Aposkopousa. The type, most commonly associated with Pan and the
satyrs, gets its name from the gesture of shading the eyes with
the hand to assist distant vision. Curiously enough, in Greek art
such a natural gesture is far from general. 'Auf keinem einzigen
mutterländischen Monument ist uns ein spähender Olympier
begegnet', reported Dr. Ines Jucker [3], and she kindly informs me
by letter that she has still (August 1960) found no exception for
Greece. I shall do no more than observe that ὀξυδερκής fits in well
with such a gesture (if one examines the context of ὀξέα δερκόμενος
at Hom. Hymn. xix (Pan), 14 and ὀξυδερκέστατα at Lucian *Philo-
patr.* 19) [4] and turn again to the 'cautionary' tale.

would be special point in the use of ὄθομαι: 'For you he will have a little
respect in his 'regarders' . . . , but for me he has no regard at all'.
[1] *Le sanctuaire d'Apollon pythéen á Argos*, Paris 1956; cf. *B.C.H.* 31
(1907), 148 ff., 159 ff.
[2] *R.E.G.* 70 (1957), 484. Vollgraff (*op. cit.*, pp. 77-84) assigns the tholos,
just east of the terrace of Apollo, to Leto. He dates the temple of Athene at
not later than the third quarter of the sixth century.
[3] *Der Gestus des Aposkopein*, Zürich 1956, p. 122.
[4] Cf. Luc. *Saturn.* 18 ὁ οἰνοχόος ὀξὺ δεδορκέτω ἐκ περιωπῆς ἐς ἕκαστον . . .

The character of Pherekydes' version

We shall open with a question which is incapable of complete answer, but which best leads into my interpretation of the *Bath of Pallas*: Why did Kallimachos write the composition? An earlier generation was confident that it knew the answer; it was written specifically for the Argive festival. This is the basic assumption of, for example, F. Susemihl in his *Geschichte der gr. Lit. in der Alexandrinerzeit* (I [1891], p. 358: 'ohne Zweifel') and A. Couat in his *Poésie Alexandrine* (1882). Although subsequently scholars have rejected the idea that the movements of any of the hymns were designed to dovetail with the actual schedule of a festival procession, or even that a specific performance of any festival lies behind the production, it is still possible for the unwary student to run foul of works in which a festival is assumed to be the raison d'être of one or other of the hymns. With what results for the evaluation of H. 5 we may see from Cahen's edition of Kallimachos in the Budé series (4th ed. 1953):

> 'The Callimachean hymn is not simply a literary diversion. If none of these pieces appears to have been recited *in the course* of a religious ceremony, each of them (with the exclusion of Hymn I) is applied and adapted to a particular festival or ritual, and is not intelligible apart from them'. (p. 204)
> 'In this kind of composition the tableau is not a pretext to tell the story: it is the tableau which forms the real subject—here the Argive festival—while the story, whatever its extent—here the story of Teiresias—fills only a pause in the ceremony. The work is satisfying from an artistic point of view only when tableau and story form a complete unity, the story expressing the very sentiment which springs from the ritual situation.' (p. 285; cf. *Callimaque*, pp. 276-7).

Students will hardly feel encouraged to take further interest in Kallimachos when they discover that, on Cahen's premises,

> 'C'est même le défaut de sa pièce que les deux éléments, tableau et récit, ne sont pas bien fondus dans une même impression. L'histoire tragique du futur devin n'a guère à faire avec le sentiment général, plutôt doux et gracieux, qui anime le tableau rituel: la narration s'enchaîne sur un détail, non sur une impression d'ensemble qui l'appelle. (p. 286) [1].

I have no illusions that every reader will respond favourably to Kallimachos' art, but let us not multiply difficulties unneces-

---

[1]   Further grievances against H. 5 in *Callimaque*, pp. 310, 604. Cf. Kuiper, *Studia Callimachea*, II p. 49, who writes that the Teiresias story is 'tenui profecto filo consuta cum Palladis cultu Argivo'.

sarily. I say 'unnecessarily', because the important question is
whether it was the poet's own idea to write the composition, or
whether it was not merely a personal challenge, but one issued by
some contemporary embodiment of the whispering Phthonos of
Hymn 2:

> 'So Kallimachos fancies himself as a writer of hymns? It hardly calls for
> real ingenuity to extol a divinity's exaction of a just vengeance. We are
> in fact a little tired of the hymn that sings of a god's or goddess's favourite,
> or of punishment meted out to the irreligious or the sacrilegious. You have
> been stuffily traditional in this regard yourself (H. 3.183 ff., 260 ff.). What
> of a divine favourite who suffers terribly and seemingly inexplicably?
> What of an unwitting offender and a punishment which far exceeds the
> crime? Now it happens that I know of just such a tragic tale . . .'

Of course we shall never know the answer, but I hope that, when
we find a real occasion to ask such a question, it is obvious that
it is the 'cautionary' tale which dictates the treatment, and not
the pseudo-religious frame into which the tale is inserted. It is
as well to remember that Kallimachos does not allow traditional
respect for the pantheon to interfere with his art. He has no intention whatever of proselytising in Athene's interest. He intends
to tell a good, and a clever, story and at the same time to bring new
life to a number of traditional forms. I mentioned the Pherecydean
version as a challenge. Commentators have tended to lose sight
of the thoroughly unpromising material which it could provide
for a Hellenist. A savage tale which satisfied a more primitive
mentality which did not grade offences, and was more concerned
with the 'How?' than the 'Why?', was by no means automatically
excluded from the repertoire of a polymath who constantly would
encounter the odd and the bizarre. But the moment that Kallimachos' learned audience realised that the poet was going to relate
this version of the story of Teiresias, they must have been more than
a little curious to know how he was going to make so crude and
insensitive a tale *conform to the requirements of a laudatory hymn,
presented in a metre which had become standard for the display of Hellenistic grace and elegance of expression.* Even when using the epic
medium Hellenistic poets went through at least the motions of
apologizing for using crude material [1]; how much more should we
expect it in an elegiac hymn.

It is possible to draw a parallel. We are told in the Old Testament

---

[1] Ap. Rhod. *Arg.* IV. 984; Arat. 637. Cf. Kuiper, *Studia Callimachea,*
II pp. 153-4.

(2 Sam. 6⁶) that, for what would seem to many today the laudable
act of steadying the Ark, Uzzah experienced the anger of Yahweh
and was struck dead. There are doubtless many neo-Hellenists
who would ignore the light thrown on such a statement by Comparative Religion, and content themselves with a bland 'The things
they used to swallow in those days', or militantly regard it as an
obstacle to religious belief of any sort. With what sort of feelings
would such a man compose (and his friends read) *a psalm upon the
subject*? Understand it, he could not or would not; he must therefore either turn to burlesque or, transforming the incident, show us
how it really happened.

I suspect that it would be difficult for the *literati* of the third
century B.C. to imagine a more innocuous offence than the accidental sight of a goddess at her bath. With the loss of the intensity
of religious feeling which gave meaning to the offence [1], the sin
became trivial, likely to cause embarrassment, but not outrage.
Ovid, for one, reflects such an attitude to the misdemeanour
(*Met.* 3, 141-2):

At bene si quaeras, Fortunae crimen in illo,
   non scelus inuenies, quod enim scelus error habebat?

Kallimachos then is dealing with highly unpromising material,
material which must be given an original twist if it is not to convey—
instead of the goddess's power (as in the traditional aretalogy)—
the goddess's caprice and perversity. Before the Pherecydean tale
the poet might have echoed Poseidon's words to Athene at Eur.
Troad. 67-8:

τί δ' ὧδε πηδᾷς ἄλλοτ' εἰς ἄλλους τρόπους
μισεῖς τε λίαν καὶ φιλεῖς ὃν ἂν τύχῃς;

And yet his first readers might have felt that the poet was making
the task doubly difficult by laying such strong emphasis on the
piteousness of the situation; this must have seemed to commit him
irrevocably to the savagery and indelicacy of the primitive tale.
In point of fact the reader who early became alive to the presence
of Athene Oxyderkes might feel that the poet was extending himself still further, by recalling a divinity remembered for her love for

---

[1]   For the irrelevance in early Greek thought of whether sin was committed
deliberately or unwittingly, see Mair, Hastings' *E.R.E.* 11. 546. He compares
the case of Oineus at *Il.* 9. 533 ff.

her favourite and for the improvement of his eyesight. In retrospect it will be discovered that this is precisely why he attaches the tale to Oxyderkes, for she is a goddess from whom one might expect that, if she had to punish, she would naturally punish through the eyes and would, equally naturally, not fail to leave her favourite with some form of consolation; but before the plan was detected there would, I suspect, have been much scratching of heads.

I have mentioned the savagery of the Pherecydean story. We have always to bear in mind that Kallimachos did not owe his knowledge of this tale to the lacunose text of pseudo-Apollodoros, as we do, but to the text of Pherekydes itself. There is good reason to believe that at one important point the two texts differed. The Apollodoran account of the blinding is expressed in this form: τὴν δὲ ταῖς χερσὶ τοὺς ὀφθαλμοὺς αὐτοῦ καταλαβομένην πηρὸν ποιῆσαι. It is useful to notice Frazer's comment on the passage:

> 'These words have been wrongly suspected or altered by the editors. Heyne proposed to omit τοὺς ὀφθαλμοὺς as a gloss or to rewrite the passage thus: τὴν δὲ ταῖς χερσὶ τῶν ὀφθαλμῶν αὐτοῦ ὕδωρ καταβαλοῦσαν πηρὸν ποιῆσαι. Hercher wrote: τὴν δὲ ταῖς χερσὶ τῶν ὀφθαλμῶν αὐτοῦ λαβομένην πηρὸν ποιῆσαι. They all apparently suppose that the goddess blinded Teiresias by scratching out his eyes. But she simply held her hands over the eyes of the prying intruder, and the mere touch of her divine fingers sufficed to blind him for ever.'

For the usage of the verb he compares Plato *Theaetetus* 165 B-C, including καταλαβὼν τῇ χειρὶ σοῦ τὸν ἕτερον ὀφθαλμόν, and for the middle voice Diod. Sic. 3. 37. 5 κατελάβοντο δεσμοῖς τὸ στόμιον, of stopping up the mouth of a snake's lair. Liddell-Scott-Jones add Plut. *Sert.* 26, in which the sense is 'held down' rather than 'covered': (Antonius) περιπεσὼν εἰς τὸ στῆθος (Sertorii) κατέλαβε τὰς χεῖρας ἀμφοτέρας.

I should prefer to read 'unwitting offender' for 'prying intruder', but a more serious ground for complaint is Frazer's failure to see that, if Spanheim, Heyne, Hercher and the rest believed that Athene tore out Teiresias' eyes, they are in the best of company. For Kallimachos makes studied use of the feature. Teiresias 'is no longer to take away his eyes' (81); Chariklo laments that Athene has 'snatched away' her son's eyes (87); Helikon 'keeps, holds' her son's eyes (92); Athene replies that it is not her pleasure to 'snatch away' children's eyes (99-100). In three of these four cases we may toy with the translation 'eyesight', but line 92 is quite unequivocal: ‹ὦ Ἑλικὼν . . . .› φάεα παιδὸς ἔχεις. Moreover the structure suggests that in Athene's 'comfortable words' the quest of Aktaion's mother for her son's bones (115-6) is to be weighed against line 92; Helikon has *only* Teiresias' eyes. And Nonnos, who draws freely upon Kallimachos when narrating the downfall of Aktaion, uses language which is hardly appropriate to merely a divine touch. Teiresias is fortunate to have got off so lightly; 'would that Artemis too, like Athene, had *attacked* (ἐπέχραεν) my eyes', says Aktaion on his deathbed (*Dion.* 5. 344-5). We may rest assured that Athene did in fact gouge out Teiresias' eyes.

And yet καταλαβομένην cannot express this idea. It must be taken as Frazer took it, 'cover'. Nor is there justification for our changing the text. The explanation of this curious situation has, I believe, been indirectly provided by Dr. van der Valk [1]. In a long and detailed discussion of [Apollodoros]' sources, including Pherekydes, he comments on the squeamishness of the author in the face of crude material, and his attempts to make the stories more acceptable to contemporary taste. Whether the bowdlerization is really thoroughgoing enough to allow us to follow van der Valk's suggestion that the *Bibliotheca* was intended as a school textbook, is another question; but there can be no doubt that [Apollodoros] did react to unsavoury versions, and that Pherekydes was an author who had given him occasion for emendation. Van der Valk does not discuss the story of Teiresias from this point of view [2], but there seems to me abundant reason to suspect that καταλαβομένην is another improvement upon the text of Pherekydes. But while pseudo-Apollodoros might make his peace with gentility in this way, Kallimachos would have to face the uncompromising eye-gouging of the original version.

TEIRESIAS

The first thing that strikes the eye in the Teiresias episode is that Kallimachos devotes no fewer than eleven lines (57-67) to a simple idea: 'Chariklo was Athene's favourite'. At the close of the episode he devotes twelve lines (119-130) to the benefits which Teiresias received from Athene. There is a balance here that is quite deliberate. It is not simply a question of counting lines, but above all of emotional content. At the opening of the tale we

[1] *R.E.G.* 71 (1958), 100-168.
[2] See *op. cit.* p. 164 and n. 235.

are encouraged to pity Chariklo. Notice, for example, that in the
Hymn to Demeter—in which we find a similar structure, but a cautionary tale treated in a spirit of burlesque, because Erysichthon
cannot be pitied—Demeter's love for Triopas, the offender's father,
is dismissed in *half a line*: 'And the goddess was as passionately
fond (ἐπεμαίνετο) of the place as she was of Eleusis, *and of Triopas
as much as she was of the nymph Enna*' (29-30). Moreover Demeter's
love is shared; so Triopas is expressly relegated to the position of
local favourite. In H. 6 that love is expressed through the curt
ἐπεμαίνετο, in H. 5 through the whole of line 58: πουλύ τι καὶ πέρι δὴ
φίλατο τᾶν ἑταρᾶν, without, moreover, any suggestion in the latter
place that the goddess divides her affection. Now in the hands of an
orthodox writer of hymns Demeter's love for Triopas and Athene's
love for Chariklo are commensurate themes, but Kallimachos pays
attention to the emotions that the exposition of such love should
kindle in us. The coverage that he gives to the subject in H. 5 *formally* makes such love deep and warm; we are supposed to share in
it, and be moved to pity and revulsion at the thought of what the
favourite is to suffer at the goddess's hands. But in H. 6 the love
seems considerably colder, rather a terse historical verdict, through
being sketched so rapidly; we are not invited to share in it, for
Erysichthon's situation is irremediable.

Now this is a strange opening to a cautionary tale. Divinities
may reasonably be no respecters of persons, but it is one thing to
stress the justice of a divine act, quite another to sidetrack the
emotions of the reader into pity and concern for an innocent third
party. And yet Kallimachos maintains this atmosphere. The eleven
lines on Athene's love for Chariklo are followed by the arresting
warning: 'But many a tear still awaited even her, although the
congenial companion of Athene'. Then the poet sets the stage for
the crime. Athene and Chariklo were bathing in the spring Hippokrene on Mt. Helikon. 'A midday calm rested on the mountain.
Both were bathing, and it was the midday hour, and a great calm
rested on that mountain'. Even in a translation which does not
attempt to do justice to the sonority of the original, it is possible
to appreciate the way in which Kallimachos has strengthened his
image by the use of double lines. 'Un effet littéraire', rightly says
Couat [1], 'et des plus heureux'. No less rightly Cahen: "Un effet

---

[1]   *La Poésie Alexandrine*, p. 285 n. 2.

lyrique, comme d'une melodie qui se renforce en se variant' [1].

Teiresias is a figure of Theban mythology, therefore a Boeotian locale must be found for the noontide bath. Kallimachos thinks of Hippokrene, the celebrated spring created by the hoof of Pegasos, the source of inspiration for poets, and of Helikon, the home of the Muses, the scene of Hesiod's commissioning as a poet. Those who are interested in winning debating points will learn from Wilamowitz [2] that Hippokrene is both unprepossessing and cannot be bathed in; that, moreover, the injunctions in lines 45-6 to stop drawing water from the Inachos ignore the fact that the Argives did not draw water from the river, 'wo auch nicht viel zu holen war'. There are, to be sure, occasions on which we need Gomme's general reminder at *C.R.* 39 (1925), 101, that the Greek, modern and ancient, draws a sharp distinction between clear spring and turbid river; that 'no Greek, if he can help it, drinks from a river'. But Wilamowitz carries his observations beyond the stage of interesting sidelight. It is a little amusing to be told by him that the situation of Hippokrene made it no natural place for a goddess to choose for her bath. Even a resident of the district, Hesiod, thought otherwise (*Theog.* 5-6). Kallimachos may reasonably assume that what was good enough for the Muses of Helikon was good enough for Athene [3].

'Bathing . . . midday . . . calm . . bathing . . midday . . calm'. But to a Greek this is no image of serenity. There is an atmosphere of foreboding, the lull before the storm. For this is the hour at which contact with divinities, whether greater or lesser, is both most likely and most perilous [4]. The belief is widespread in Greek folklore, both ancient and modern. It is accordingly assumed that it was at midday that Hesiod met the Muses [5], but then he was in the enviable position of Chariklo, not that of Teiresias. This

---

[1] *Callimaque*, p. 560.

[2] *Hell. Dicht.* II pp. 19-20.

[3] Cahen (*Comm.*, 229) is at first inclined to accept the fact that the Inachos dries up in winter (Paus. ii. 15, 5) as evidence that the ritual bath occurred at another time of the year. But there is a good deal to be said for his second thoughts: 'Ou bien on verra encore ici la preuve que c'est la mystique ἐπιδημία que retrace ici le poète, plus qu'une pratique rituelle effective'.

[4] For exx. see Gow ad Theocr. 1. 15-18; Frazer ad Ov. *Fast.* iv. 761; Rohde, *Psyche* (trans. W. B. Hillis, 1925), pp. 323, 592-3; especially Kleinknecht, pp. 328-9. Not unnaturally Artemis' bath (Ov. *Fast.* iv. 761; *Met.* 3, 144 f., 151 f.) occurs at the same hour.

[5] *Anth. Pal.* ix. 64.

is not the only place in the hymn where the poet transforms an image by focusing our attention on the associations of a single word, for we shall notice the same device in line 17. Here then the music speaks of calm, but sinister midday prepares us for disaster.

Teiresias is presented to us through his mother's eyes. He is firstly ἔτι μῶνος. This has been variously translated. Some (e.g. Cahen and Couat) translate 'alone', as if ἔτι does not matter. Others give the words a wider function in the sentence: 'Only Teiresias . . . still ranged with his hounds the holy place' (Mair); 'Nur Teiresias noch . . . strich mit den Hunden umher nahe dem heiligen Ort' (Howald-Staiger). But the studied parallelism between the situations of Teiresias and Aktaion suggests to me that ἔτι μῶνος is the equivalent of τὸν μόνον παῖδα in 108-9, that is, 'still an only child'. He is furthermore in the bloom of youth, ἄρτι γένεια περκάζων, in other words, κοῦρος . . . πρῶτον ὑπηνήτης, τοῦ περ χαριεστάτη ἥβη (Il. 24.347-8). Perhaps it was because in the closely knit Greek family sons were the promise of support [1] for parents in their old age that the Greeks were particularly conscious of the tragedy of a blighted life. As a remarkable example we may notice the way in which the Nekyia invests even the young upstart giants Otos and Ephialtes with the pathos which attaches to tragic waste: Apollo destroyed them both

$$\pi\rho\text{ί}ν \ \sigma\varphi\omega\text{ϊ}ν \ \text{ὑ}π\text{ὸ} \ \varkappa\rho\text{ο}\tau\text{ά}\varphi\text{ο}\iota\sigma\iota\nu \ \text{ἰ}\text{ο}\text{ύ}\lambda\text{ο}\text{υ}\text{ς}$$
$$\text{ἀ}\nu\theta\tilde{\eta}\sigma\alpha\iota \ \pi\text{υ}\varkappa\text{ά}\sigma\alpha\iota \ \tau\varepsilon \ \gamma\text{έ}\nu\text{υ}\text{ς} \ \varepsilon\text{ὐ}\alpha\nu\theta\text{έ}\text{ϊ} \ \lambda\text{ά}\chi\nu\eta.$$

And then Teiresias' presence at the spring is dictated by a most natural and pardonable motive, extreme thirst. His offence is accidental, the tragic error. And for all her anger, Athene pities him. But blindness follows. Throughout all this the language is tender and delicate. Teiresias 'saw what it was not lawful to see'; 'night covered the lad's eyes'. We must pity Teiresias; the poet insists upon it.

Teiresias' agony renders him speechless, a consummate touch. For however natural his aphasia may be in terms of nervous reaction, it is far more important from a dramatic point of view. Teiresias must not be allowed to speak. He is too deeply committed

---

[1] θρέπτρα Il. 4. 478, 17. 302; θρεπτήρια Hes. Works and Days 188. Peek's collection of verse inscriptions swarms with expressions such as γηροτρόφοι ἐλπίδες, φροντὶς γηροκόμος (1420. 10, 1519. 8).

in the situation to be able to make any comment which would not complicate matters considerably, and embarrass Athene in her (as yet undisclosed) sympathetic handling of the situation. We know what we would have said, and the realism of Kallimachos would have obliged him to say it too, if it had been part of his artistic purpose. In the sixth hymn the favourite's son speaks—and tells Demeter to 'shove off or I'll stick my big axe in your skin'; at that Nemesis pricks up her ears and the future pattern of Erysichthon's wretched life is determined.

By way of an aside, we may illustrate the way in which the poet is artistically assembling his material by the parallels which Klein-knecht (p. 329 n. 3) introduces, when discussing lines 83-4. He compares Hom. Hymn. 2 (*Dem.*) 281-2 τῆς (Metaneira) δ' αὐτίκα γούνατ' ἔλυντο, δηρὸν δ' ἄφθογγος γένετο χρόνον and, more generally, the description of the attendants in H. 6. 59 as ἡμιθνῆτες. Now in both of these cases the victims are confronted with a revelation of divinity, an epiphany. But in H. 5 things are different. There are no awe-inspiring dimensions, no divine fragrance, brightness or beauty. Nor is Teiresias Saul on the Damascus road, or Epizelos of Athens, stricken with blindness 'without blow of sword or dart' when he saw a gigantic phantom at Marathon (Hdt. 6. 117). His eyes are torn out, he goes into a state of shock. We have moved a long way from the earlier products of piety. And even in H. 6 the reaction of Erysichthon's attendants to the revelation of Demeter's stature is controlled by the playwright. They are 'half dead' (with fear, cf. Aeschin. 3. 159), but they are puppets in Kallimachos' hands. He wants them out of the road, and so their legs are as nimble as ever, ἐξαπίνας ἀπόρουσαν. The machinery of divine action is being mani-pulated to suit the poet's purpose.

Teiresias is speechless, and so Chariklo must intercede for him, for the relationship of love exists between her and Athene. The nymph of course is astounded and furious: 'Lady, what have you done to my boy? Is this the sort of friends you goddesses are? You have taken away my lad's eyes. Ill-starred child, you have seen Athene's breast and flanks, but you shall not see the sun again. Ah, wretch that I am. Oh Mt. Helikon, that I may no longer tra-verse, you have exacted great things in exchange for small. For the loss of a few roes and deer you hold the eyes of my boy.'

Now nothing is clearer to me than that Kallimachos is not going to wreck a poem on which he has expended so much effort by indulging in the preciosity and bad taste of which Cahen [1] convicts him in this passage. He has not paid enough attention to Couat's good comment on the difference between the delicate phraseology of the narrator at lines 78 and 82 and the unadorned language of Chariklo at lines 87-88, describing the same events:

> 'Il est vrai que cette délicatesse ne se retrouve plus dans le discours de la mère de Tirésias. Elle n'est pas tellement égarée par la douleur qu'elle ne puisse encore jouer sur les mots et faire de piquantes antithèses'. [2]

If Couat's respect here for the craftsmanship of the poet is well founded, it would be curious if Kallimachos was prepared to ruin his effects by injudicious pedantry in the same passage. Let us look at it in more detail.

Howald-Staiger suggested that Chariklo's address to the mountain is motivated by fear of upbraiding Athene direct. Perhaps, but this is not among the most important considerations. We notice firstly the sudden change of subject—Athene, Teiresias, Helikon— surely intended to reflect Chariklo's distraction; we should remember the emotional changes of subject in lines 1-4. Again, the apostrophe to the mountain has good tragic precedent. We remember above all blinded Oidipus' apostrophe to Kithairon, featuring the same emotional changes of subject: ἰὼ Κιθαιρών . . . ὦ Πόλυβε κτλ . . . ὦ τρεῖς κέλευθοι κτλ . . . . . . ὦ γάμοι γάμοι . . . . (Soph. *O.T.* 1391 ff.) [3] 'When people cannot be trusted or do not understand, nature personified provides comfort'. [1] Again, as Kleinknecht (p. 325) acutely observed, the important thing is that Chariklo utters reproachful laments at all, for the Pherecydean story contained a plea for the repair of Teiresias' eyesight, and this has been replaced by the poet with the reproaches. By this device Athene's generosity is entirely unprompted, and we feel deeper respect for the goddess's compassion.

Furthermore we may use the eye motif provided by Athene

---

[1] Budé edition, p. 287.

[2] *Poés. alex.*, p. 288.

[3] Cf. Eur. *Herc. Fur.* 887-893: ἰὼ μοι μέλεος, ἰὼ Ζεῦ . . . ., ἰὼ στέγαι, ... ἰὼ δόμοι. A large number of examples of the apostrophe of nature as a dramatic device are collected by A. P. Wagener, *T.A.P.A.* 62 (1931), 78-100. Cf. F. L. Shisler, *T.A.P.A.* 73 (1942), 282-3. For personification and animation of nature as a Euripidean specialty Kleinknecht (p. 331 n. 3) refers to W. Schadewaldt, *Monolog und Selbstgespräch*, *N.Ph.U.* 2 (1926) and W. Breitenbach, *Untersuchungen zur Sprache der euripideischen Lyrik*, Tüb. Beitr. 20 (1934).

[4] G. Luck, *The Latin Love Elegy*, p. 27 n.1.

Oxyderkes to give special point to lines 91-2, which are usually translated in this way: 'You have driven a hard bargain for so small a loss. For the loss of a few roes and deer you hold the eyes of my lad.' Now Chariklo is not only furious, she is also bitter. She expected better things of her relationship with Athene. The key to her asperity is provided by δόρκας. At H. 3. 97 and fr. 676. 1 Kallimachos uses the etymologically purer form in zeta [1], ζόρξ (cf. ζόρκας in Herodotos), precisely because it is the rarer form. Here he uses the common form in delta, δόρξ (cf. Attic δορκάς), not just because it is simpler (and therefore suits the elegiac medium better), but because the form enshrined a popular etymology which he wanted to utilize. This animal (the roe in Greece, the gazelle in Syria and Africa) received its name—we all too easily forget—from its large eyes (δέρκομαι, δέδορκα). The mountain which has lost a few of its large eyes has gained Teiresias' tiny pair—contrary to expectation, μεγάλ' ἀντ' ὀλίγων. An interesting example of the *ius talionis*, an eye for an eye. Admittedly Kallimachos is running a risk on this occasion, for it is easy to doubt that what could be construed as an engaging verbal play could at the same time be remotely natural to a mother's grief. I think that it can, granted the intensity of the mother's bitterness, but Kallimachos treads a tightrope. Perhaps in fact we are encouraged to make a concession by the sound of these lines. As I read them aloud I am struck by the combinations of omicron with the liquids: ὀλίγων . . . δόρκας ὀλέσσας . . . πρόκας οὐ πολλάς. Is it reading too much into these to hear in them the shrill notes of an ὀλολυγή? [2]

There is good reason for making allowances at this place, and

---

[1] See Frisk, Hofmann s.v.; Chantraine, *Formation des noms*, p. 3.

[2] Cf. ὄλολοι = δεισιδαίμονες Theopomp. Com. 61, Men. 112. For the onomatopoeia of ὀλολυγή, ὀλολυγών, *ululare*, etc., see S. G. Oliphant, *T.A.P.A.* 47 (1916), 103. The common element covers 'almost any howl, shriek, or piercing cry'. For the effect, cf. Aesch. *Ag.* 595 (cf. 587-9) ὀλολυγμὸν ἄλλος ἄλλοθεν κατὰ πτόλιν; Rhianos *Anth. Pal.* vi 173. 3 γαλλαίῳ Κυβέλης ὀλολύγματι πολλάκι. A glance at Italie's indices to Aeschylus and Euripides will suggest that *ol-* in a lugubrious context attracts other examples to itself. E.g. (ἀπ)όλλυμι and δόλος/δόλιος (Aesch. *Cho.* 888, Eur. *El.* 154, *Herc. Fur.* 754), (ἀπ)όλλυμι and πόλις (Aesch. *Ag.* 1167, Eur. *Troad.* 1078, *Herc. Fur.* 1055, *Supp.* 191-2 πόλεις πολλαὶ διώλοντο) and other combinations (e.g. Aesch. *Eum.* 1043, *Sept.* 825). Cf. also Hom. *Od.* 10.132 αὐτὰρ αἱ ἄλλαι ἀολλέες αὐτόθ' ὄλοντο; Ap. Rh. *Arg.* 4.485 Κόλχον δ' ὄλεκον στόλον. For something similar note Van Groningen, *Poésie verbale grecque*, p. 70, on Philitas fr. 7.3 νέαι αἰὲν ἀνῖαι, 'qui fait indirectement résonner à nos oreilles un αἰαῖ impressionnant'.

that is the interesting turn of events. Up to this point the whole of our pity has been orientated towards first Chariklo, then Teiresias. When the nymph throws her arms about her son and γοερᾶν οἶτον ἀηδονίδων ἆγε βαρὺ κλαίοισα (94-5), a seal seems to be set upon the traditional savagery of the tale, and salvage seems impossible. The more so, as in 94-5 the poet has welded together the lament of the nightingale for her mutilated son and the account of Kleopatra at *Il.* 9. 563, called Halkyone by her parents because her μήτηρ ἀλκυόνος πολυπενθέος οἶτον ἔχουσα | κλαῖεν ὅ μιν ἑκάεργος ἀνήρπασε Φοῖβος ’Απόλλων. (Interestingly enough, both nightingale and kingfisher are birds whose lament is described as an *elegos*.) [1] But now a surprising thing happens. The goddess justifies her action. Opstelten (*Sophocles and Greek Pessimism*, p. 100) drew our attention to a particular point in the *Ajax*:

> 'The fact that in the darkness of the hero's madness Athena almost playfully smites down his heroism makes us realize, with a feeling of shock, the contrast between the insignificance of the magnivolent hero, on the one hand, and the deity, on the other, *who does not need to give an account of herself.*' (My italics)

We may contrast the humanity of Kallimachos' Athene. She declares that she has not blinded Teiresias, that she does not think it pleasant to rob children of their eyes. 'But thus state the laws of Kronos: "Whoever sees a god when the god himself does not choose, pays dearly for the sight" [2].' We may safely assume that Pherekydes had not attempted to explain Athene's savage action; it is left for Kallimachos to justify, by the simple expedient of invoking Draconic laws of Kronos.

Kronos here clearly is not the ruler of the Golden Age, but is true to the character given to him in Hesiod's *Theogony*—most terrible of Earth's children, hater and mutilator of his father, swallower of his children. He is not only the representative of an earlier generation than the members of the pantheon, but also the symbol of a cruder, more barbaric age which still binds the

---

[1] Ar. *Av.* 209 ff.; Eur. *I.T.* 1089 ff. Cf. Page, *Greek Poetry and Life* (Essays Gilbert Murray), p. 208. Notice also, to refer back to the subject of the previous note, that the ὀλολυγών also has a lament (although we do not really know whether we should credit the creature with a hoot or a croak): ὀλολυγόνος οἶτον ἔχουσα, | Βυβλὶς . . . ὠδύρατο (Nikainetos fr. 1. 9-10 Powell).

[2] Kleinknecht pertinently compares χρησμοὶ τῶν ‘Ελληνικῶν θεῶν 44, 5 (Buresch, *Klaros*, 1889, p. 108): θνητοῖς γὰρ χαλεπὸν φύσιν ἄμβροτον ὀφθαλμοῖσιν | εἰσιδέειν, ἢν μή τις ἔχῃ σύνθημα θέειον.

humane household of Zeus against their will. This being so, the slip of F. L. Lucas (*Greek Poetry for Everyman*, p. 301) could not be more unfortunate: 'But thus the solemn edict of the *Son of Cronus* lies—'.

Mention of the Fates increases the pathos. Not only is Athene committed to penalizing Teiresias, but she could not have avoided the encounter, however great her powers of foresight. For his destiny had been spun from the moment of his birth; the Fates *fatalia nentes stamina, non ulli dissoluenda deo* [1], weave a web which 'no man, brave or coward, has escaped, once he has been born' [2].

One thing cannot be overstressed. The invocation of the laws of Kronos is a master stroke, for we now find ourselves taking what seems to me the unprecedented step of *pitying the goddess*, in a hymn which started out on a much grimmer note, added the pathos of lament as if the suffering of the goddess's favourite was somehow to glorify the divinity, and then canalized all the pity towards the goddess herself. *Teiresias* οὐκ ἐθέλων *gives place to Athene* οὐκ ἐθέλουσα. This not only solves the problem of how Athene committed such an act; it also makes it possible to preserve a formal harmony between myth and hymn. No impediment obstructs our venerating the goddess, and the rest of the episode is designed to increase our admiration for Athene. At this point in the story Kallimachos' hands were to a certain extent bound. The Pherecydean story committed him to the irrevocability of Teiresias' blinding and at the same time to benefits conferred by Athene. But there was still opportunity for the poet to introduce a refinement into the story. I presume that originally Athene tore out Teiresias' eyes, then took pity on Chariklo in her distress and sought to make restitution to Teiresias by her gifts. Kallimachos, having made Athene no traitor to her humane nature over the blinding, would go further and demonstrate that Athene showed her humanity in the very form in which she punished Teiresias. And so the convenient law of Kronos is phrased so as to allow discretion to the offended deity—the offender 'shall pay dearly for the sight'.

Here we may learn from others' inattention. Athene does *not* say what Prof. Grimal [3] attributes to her, 'que tout mortel qui

---

[1] Tibull. V. 1-2.

[2] *Il.* 6. 488-9.

[3] *Dict. de la myth. gr. et rom.* s.v. Chariclo 3. The same error in Frazer, *Apollodorus* (Loeb edtn.) I p. 363 n. 1.

voyait un immortel contre la volonté de celui-ci, devait perdre l'usage de la vue'. In lines 51-4, to be sure, this is declared the fate awaiting the unwitting male who sees *Athene* at her bath, but that thought is prompted by the figure of Athene Oxyderkes. Nor can 101-2 be cited as evidence that 'to see any deity uninvited brings destruction' (H. J. Rose, *Oxford Class. Dict.* s.v. Actaeon). The whole point of the formula is that it must cover the punishments of both Teiresias and Aktaion, blinding as well as destruction. We see further that, if the blinding of Teiresias in Pherekydes' version ever was an exercise of the *ius talionis* (womit man sündigt, daran wird man gestraft') [1], the motive has been completely transformed by Kallimachos.

Before we look at the Aktaion story, it is as well to point out that Kallimachos has not quite perfect control over the change from Pherekydes' version, although it is a minor defect and not really obvious. If Athene's humanity is evident in the form of punishment inflicted on Teiresias, then the pity she feels for Chariklo in line 95 is really retrospective—it includes the prior punishment as well as the *apologia* and the forthcoming gifts. But the poet has kept the order of Pherekydes, in whom the goddess's pity links two clearly defined and capricious moods, Athene's brutality and Athene's compassion.

AKTAION

In lines 107-118 the poet introduces his own version of the story of Aktaion, to illustrate the fact that two goddesses could react quite differently, according to their natures, when the 'law of Kronos' had to be observed. It has long been recognized that the version in which Aktaion surprised Artemis at her bath does not occur before the time of Kallimachos, but springs into prominence thereafter [2]. It would not be surprising if our poet was wholly responsible for it. He wishes to show how even so brutal

---

[1] Kleinknecht, p. 324. He is followed by H. Hunger, *Lexikon der gr. und röm. myth.*[5] (1959), p. 339.

[2] See S. Reinach, *Cultes, Mythes et Religions* III (1908), 24-53. There is no need for me to venture into the question of the original form of the Aktaion story. For this debated question see Robert, *Gr. Heldensage*, p. 127; Wilamowitz, *Hell. Dicht.* II pp. 23 ff.; T. Zielinski, *Eos* 29 (1926), 1-7 (= *Iresione* II (1936), 268-275); Fr. Marx, 'Aktaion', *Berichte der sächs. Ges. der Wiss.* 58. 101 ff.; L. Radermacher, *Mythos und Sage bei den Griechen* (1938), pp. 51-2; Kleinknecht, pp. 336-7.

an act can excite our sympathy for the goddess and justify traditional respect for her. And so he uses Artemis and Aktaion as a foil.

We may guess that it was the total dismemberment of Aktaion in the current versions which first drew his attention to the possibilities of the story, and allowed the bones of Aktaion on the mountain to be set against the eyes of Teiresias on Helikon. [1] We may also guess that it was because there was a difference of opinion on the nature of Aktaion's offence that Kallimachos felt entitled to enter the lists as the champion of a new theory. For Aktaion was reported to have boasted of being a better hunter than Artemis [2], to have dared to make love to her [3] or to have sought to marry Semele, in whom Zeus had a current interest. [4] Now if the contrast with Athene's humanity was to be made as effective as possible, the contrasting story needed a great number of points of contact. That Aktaion should be, like Teiresias, an only child and in the bloom of youth was reasonable enough, just as there was no real obstacle to Teiresias' being a hunter, a feature imported from the Aktaion story. But above all Aktaion could not be allowed to commit his offence in a spirit of vain-glory—Athene's case would instantly fall to the ground. And so he also had to be an unconscious offender, and what better than to make him guilty of the same offence? We hear, to be sure, of others, who witnessed goddesses naked at their bath. Erymanthos, son of Apollo, was blinded because he saw Aphrodite [5]; Siproites, a hunter of Crete, was subjected to a change of sex [6], and Kalydon was changed into a mountain [7], both for seeing Artemis. But we lack the means to date the tales sufficiently to define their relationship to Kallimachos in terms of either cause or effect.

---

[1]   Cahen, keenly anxious to redeem Kallimachos from a bad reputation for antiquarianism, underlines the poet's resistance to the temptation to expatiate at length on various myths that he mentions. For the Aktaion story (*Callimaque*, p. 365) he 'passed over completely in silence' the metamorphosis of Aktaion into a stag, and various other features. The real reason is that which we shall encounter in the Eumedes episode at lines 33-42: he is not telling the story for its own sake. At the same time Cahen has missed, I think, a passing reference to metamorphosis in τὸν πρὶν ἄνακτα (114).

[2]   Eur. *Bacch.* 339.

[3]   Diodor. Sic. 4.81, 4.

[4]   Akusilaos 2 F 33 Jacoby; Stesichoros fr. 70 Edmonds.

[5]   Ptolemaios Hephaist. *Nov. Hist.* I in Westermann, *Mythographi Graeci*, p. 183.

[6]   Nikandros (?) ap. Anton. Lib. *Met.* 17. 5.

[7]   Derkyllos 288 F 1 Jacoby.

The Aktaion-Artemis story also provides Kallimachos with the opportunity to utilize a severer penalty. Autonoe and Aristaios, his parents, would make many offerings to the gods to be privileged to see their son blind, τυφλὸν ἰδέσθαι (109), a pointed juxtaposition. This is the opening thought of the episode, and it is artistically reiterated at the close of Athene's justification. Autonoe will say that you, Chariklo, are blessed and the child of fortune in receiving your child blind from the mountains. The tale also provided a closer relationship between offender and goddess, which in no way mitigated the operation of Kronos' inexorable law. Teiresias is a favourite's son, but Aktaion is a favourite himself.

The Benefits

Kallimachos now closes the Teiresias story with the list of Athene's benefits. They are carefully described as *'other'* benefits' (ἄλλα . . . γέρα), for her greatest service was Teiresias' blindness [1]. As I mentioned earlier, this catalogue combines with the introduction to the tale, of similar length, to create an artistic frame. For Athene's love for Chariklo is balanced by Athene's favour to Chariklo's son. It is interesting to notice in both sections a similar technique, by which a simple idea is finely spun throughout the pentameter: πουλύ τι καὶ πέρι δὴ φίλατο τᾶν ἑταρᾶν, 58; ἦ μέγα τῶν ἄλλων δή τι περισσότερον (122). Our summary of Pherekydes provides only two gifts, the cleansing of his hearing to understand every birdcall, and a staff of cornel wood. The former Kallimachos has rejected, perhaps because he found the idea too unsophisticated, more appropriate to a shamanistic *Melampodia*, such as Hesiod's, perhaps also because the cleansing of Teiresias' ears overlapped with the cleansing of Teiresias' vision. He proceeds instead to the commissioning of Teiresias as a seer, and then confers the skill of augury, prophecy, a staff, longevity and the retention of his wits in Hades.

The gift of augury is conveyed in language which shows a Hellenist at his technical best. One must admire the poet's dexterity in coping with the concept of birds of good omen, birds of bad omen and those of no significance for augury. We notice the variety in the presentation—the juxtaposition of singular and plural (to

---

[1] Cahen (*Comm.*, p. 241) misses the point completely with his note: 'ἄλλα = à côté de son infortune'.

avoid the sound of οἱ αἴσιοι οἵ), the extension of ἤλιθα 'in vain' (for
the augur) as 'without ulterior motive', 'with no special significance' [1], the oblique use of πτέρυγες as the instruments of flight, a
variation of the idea expressed by a verb, πέτονται, at 123. [2]

A special interest attaches, I suspect, to the gift of the staff:
δωσῶ καὶ μέγα βάκτρον, ὅ οἱ πόδας ἐς δέον ἀξεῖ (127). In the Pherecydean account it is a σκῆπτρον κράνειον (MSS. κυάνεον, corr. Aegius),
ὅ φέρων ὁμοίως τοῖς βλέπουσιν ἐβάδιζεν. A staff with magical power.
Is it still a magic staff in Kallimachos? [3] Ἐς δέον, 'according to his
need', is so vague that we are entitled to doubt it; especially if there
is the possibility of the substitution of an idea. When we find
together the commissioning of a seer on Mt. Helikon and the presentation of a staff, it would be interesting to know whether Kallimachos is making any use of Hesiod's commissioning. For it was
on Mt. Helikon (and, more specifically, at Hippokrene, according to
Kallimachos [4]) that the Muses gave the Boeotian the inspiration to
sing of things past, present and future (knowledge which is the
seer's possession), and gave him, as a badge of office, a staff (σκῆπτρον) of bay. Are we invited to contrast the practicality of Athene,
who provides no useless badge of office, but 'a staff to guide his
feet at need'?

Seercraft, augury, prophecy, staff, longevity, wisdom and standing
in Hades—the list is impressive, and intended to be so. We are
invited to recognize that Athene has made more than generous
reparation for an injury for which she was not really responsible.
In the words of Heinze (and one could wish that he had written
more on the subject): 'Wahrlich eine sehr humane Göttin, die man
herzlich lieb gewinnen muss' [5]. These words would have pleased
the poet, for I think that they reflect the thoughts that he has
worked to instil in us. And we would expect the ritual *envoi* to
occur immediately, to maintain this atmosphere. But Kallimachos
is before all else a Hellenist. He does not write with the fervour

---

[1] Mair's translation ('which is of good omen among all the countless birds
that fly') is based on the other meaning of ἤλιθα, 'very much', 'exceedingly',
and ruins the balance.

[2] Or perhaps there is a semantic shift. Cf. the use of *penna* as 'omen' in
Latin verse, e.g. at Prop. III. 10. 11 (Butler-Barber provide other examples
ad loc.).

[3] So Cahen (*Comm.*, p. 241) takes it.

[4] Fr. 112. 5-6; cf. fr. 2. 4.

[5] *Ovids Elegische Erzählung* (1919), p. 95 n. 1.

of a devotee of Athene, nor does he write for devotees. If there ever was any doubt that Kallimachos had no real interest in the Argive worship of Athene, it should have been dispelled by the way in which he shatters the atmosphere that he has created, by a deliberate piece of sophistry. Some scholars (particularly Cahen and Howald) have striven to establish that at the close of the cautionary tale in Hymn 6 Kallimachos tries to recreate the intense atmosphere of the ritual framework, to attune his audience again to the arrival of the *Kalathos*. And yet the situation there is hardly different from here, where only the mention of the bathing attendants in line 134 provides a link with the arrival of the Palladion. [1] In H. 6 it is only the mention of Demeter (116) which recalls the alleged function of the tale. Our ideas of structural harmony are not the poet's.

THE SOPHISMA

The *sophisma*, it seems to me, is a device which the poet uses in hymns in which a more intense atmosphere is generated (namely 2, 5 and 6), to remind his colleagues that he wears his religion on his sleeve, that he is personally quite uncommitted, and that a safety-valve is necessary in case they should be carried away by his emotive powers or, perhaps more likely, feel that his performance involves the jettisoning of Hellenistic principles.

Let us start with H. 2. There the epiphany is so casually developed that we find ourselves wondering whether it has taken place at all. On this question I shall show at another time that the poet is being deliberately obscurantist, to suit a purpose which can only with great difficulty be presented in the form of a short summary immediately carrying conviction. But for our present purposes it matters very little whether the epiphany really follows line 16 (Malten, Bethe, Weinreich, Herter), precedes line 97 ἰὴ ἰὴ παιῆον ἀκούομεν (Cahen; cf. Wilamowitz, *Hell. Dicht.* II 78, Howald-Staiger, p. 55) or whether Kallimachos deliberately conceals the arrival. We find in each case that the excited atmosphere created at the opening of the poem does not develop in the way which we expect. It is just not true to say that 'l'apparition du dieu est très nettement marquée', and that at line 97 (or any other line) we find 'le point d'émotion où tout marche et que tout prépare'. [2]

---

[1] Cf. L. Deubner, *N. Jbb.* 1921, p. 373 n. 1.
[2] Cahen, *Callimaque*, p. 605.

Rather, it jars upon us that the issue of so alerting an opening should be the off-handed subordination of the logical climax, an etymological explanation of the ritual cry, and a piece of literary criticism—the kicking out of Phthonos—called by Körte [1] a 'strange appendage to the hitherto harmonious unity of the *Hymn to Apollo*', which 'shows clearly enough that this disruption of harmony affords him conscious pleasure'. Yet to a great degree Körte has put the cart before the horse. In the case of H. 2 it is precisely the *lack of harmony* (which seems to persist right up to the end), coupled with a fervour rare in a Hellenistic poet, which surprise us. But the poet has complete control over his material. There *is* a mischievous *Gesichtspunkt*, a 'leg-pull' which unites the whole, and lines 1-5 and 105 ff. (principally καλῷ ποδί 3, ὁ Δήλιος φοῖνιξ 4, ποδί τ' ἤλασεν 107) are involved in it. Kallimachos sings a paean of thanksgiving to Delian Apollo, more inclined to reward than to punish (see fr. 114)—but his Delian Apollo is Ptolemy, and his Delos therefore Alexandria. By the *sophisma* at lines 3/4, therefore, the opening is divorced from genuine piety, but—a speciality of this poem—not from personal feeling. He may indulge in such warmth of expression, for the divinity whom he hymns is his king and patron.

In Hs. 5 and 6, however, no such abiding feeling is possible, for the hymns are not connected with affairs of the Court. In them the *sophisma* will simply give the lie to the sincerity of the setting.

In H. 6 I would find two *sophismata*. One is in the customary place, the end of the tale (117), where the poet deliberately destroys the effect of a pious prayer to Demeter. 'Demeter, may your enemy be no friend, or neighbour, of mine' represents a traditional saving clause, for which we find parallels, for example, at Aesch. *P.V.* 526 ff., 894 ff.; Soph. *Antig.* 372 f.; Theocr. *Id.* 26. 27-8 and Call. H. 3. 135-6. In Chapter VI we shall see that this thought itself contains a learned reference which transforms its role. But even were there nothing suspicious about it, the narrator's following remark: 'I can't stand bad neighbours' (ἐμοὶ κακογείτονες ἐχθροί) should awaken us to the possibility that the words spring from self interest rather than from a pious fear of the consequences of proximity to impiety. We are intended to see in it partly the contempt of self-righteous suburbia (in accordance with the bourgeois tone of the Erysichthon story), partly (as we shall show in Ch. VI) a

---

[1] *Hellenistic Poetry*, p. 133.

shudder at the dangers of near residence to a monster like Erysichthon. It is open to the reader to lay more emphasis on one of
these considerations than on the other, but in either case it is far
more natural that at this point the narrator continues to speak. A
narrator who is a devotee as in H. 5, but of sex appropriate to the
festival involved, the *Thesmophoria*. One thinks of an elderly woman, with an outlook reminiscent of Theokritos' fascinating
Praxinoa in *Idyll* 15.

Mention of H. 6. 116-7 provides the best moment at which to
raise the whole question of the role of the narrator in Hs. 2, 5 and 6.
Cahen (*Callimaque*, p. 396), laying emphasis on the portrayal of
collective, rather than individual, religious experience, finds the
personality of the narrator vaguely defined in *all* of Hs. 5 and 6,
and the poet as the narrator in H. 2, although there too Kallimachos
shows considerable discretion in self revelation up to the Phthonos
episode. To Howald-Staiger (p. 151), H. 5 involves a priest as
narrator, but in H. 6 the poet speaks throughout in his own person,
as in H. 2. Howald (*Der Dichter*, pp. 89-90) finds no incongruity of
thought at the close of the latter hymn. Kleinknecht (pp. 346-7)
finds anonymity ('in der vorgestellten Kultperson eines Festordners,
Chorführers, Hymnologen, Hierokeryx, oder wie wir ihn nennen
wollen') up to 2. 71, 5.55-6, 6. 116-7 and then the poet speaks in his
own person. All these views seem to me to call for some modification.

In all three hymns I take the narrator to speak throughout.
But, of course, he (or she) is a puppet who dances to the movements of her creator's hands. In the preceding pages I have tried
carefully to talk of incongruities in 'sense' or 'thought', never
incongruities of form. This is because I believe that the poet
has created hymns which are *formally* appropriate to their having
been recited *in toto* by a devotee of the divinity. Even when we
are intended to see Kallimachos' mischievous mind behind incongruities of thought, they occur in an underhand way. For example,
a devotee may, if he is so minded, legitimately explain the significance of the ritual cry ἰὴ ἰὴ παιῆον (just as the narrator in H. 5
may explain the history of the Shield of Diomedes); in both cases
we may, if *we* are so minded, think of the explanation as edifying.
Or again, an early hymn may have a *sphragis*, the personal seal of
the poet, or, if you like, the narrator may gratefully acknowledge
the assistance of Apollo; from both points of view there is nothing
formally wrong with the closing lines of H. 2. Or again, H. 6. 116-7

(if we gloss over the fact that ὁμότοιχος does not mean simply 'under the same roof') become a customary saving clause, and we may also translate 'I hate evil neighbours', which then conforms *outwardly* to the spirit of the saving clause. I am not surprised if on occasions scholars have not detected the incongruities, for there is always a formal level at which things can make sense. It is only the realisation of more than one level of reference, *always sparked by a contemporary or literary or learned allusion*, which reveals the poet's mischievous and ironical intervention.

The second *sophisma* in H. 6 must be mentioned here only briefly, for detailed discussion is better suited to my later study of Erysichthon. In Ch. VI of the present study we shall see why Kallimachos extends the hymn with an extra stanza at lines 118-128. The opening is extremely moving, a combination of credo and catechism demonstrating the simple faith of Demeter's devotees. I enlarge on the emotional content in Ch. V. The poet again draws in the reins of emotion at lines 126-7:

> ὡς δ'αἱ λικνοφόροι χρυσῷ πλέα λίκνα φέροντι,
> ὡς ἀμὲς τὸν χρυσὸν ἀφειδέα πασσαίμεσθα.

Those, like Nilsson [1], who feel surprise that the attendants are said to be bearing *likna* filled with *gold* are, I think, on the right track. Again there is the usual respect for outward appearances that I have suggested above, for Philadelphos' festival in honour of Dionysos ran absolutely riot with gold. [2] But I suspect that Kallimachos is making a verbal play in which gold and corn are equated, and it is the closing verb which provides a clue, πασσαίμεσθα, 'may we eat'. I know that scholars have emended to πᾱσαίμεσθα, 'may we get' and, most recently, πᾱσεύμεσθα, 'we shall get'; this only confirms me in my belief that here again we are dealing with a mischievous poet.

In H. 5 (lines 131-136) his *sophisma* takes the form of an *eirenicon*. He uses the opportunity to reconcile one feature of the Teiresias story as told in the Hesiodic *Melampodia* (fr. 162 Rz.) and one feature of Pherekydes' story. In the former version, the more widely circulated, Teiresias settles an argument between Zeus and Hera, by virtue of his experience both as male and female. His answer

---

[1] *Dionysiac Mysteries of the Hellenistic and Roman Age* (1957), p. 30.
[2] Kallixeinos of Rhodes (627 F 2 Jacoby) *ap.* Ath. V. 196-203 gives a long and interesting account.

humiliates Hera, and she blinds him. Zeus— *neque enim licet inrita cuiquam facta dei fecisse deo* [1]—gives him the seer's power by way of compensation. In the version which Kallimachos has followed, Athene confers the same privilege. *How can Athene lay claim to the power to bestow the same gifts as Zeus?* The question is, as we mentioned in Ch. I, *formally* a very natural one in a hymn. But the way in which Kallimachos cleverly justifies Athene's power by building upon Hesiod adds a new level of reference to these lines.

At *Theog.* 886 ff. the birth of Athene is related. Zeus took to wife Metis, 'wisest among gods and mortal men'. And when she was about to bring forth Athene, 'equal to her father in strength and wise counsel' (896), he enticed her into his belly, for Earth and Heaven had warned him that Metis would produce very wise offspring, not only Athene but also a violent son who would rule over gods and men. So Zeus put her in his belly first, 'so that the goddess might devise for him both good and evil' (900). When it was time for Athene's birth Zeus gave birth to her from his head. Now mercifully the student of Kallimachos has seldom to trouble about the first beginnings of Greek tales. There is good reason to regard our present Hesiodic story as a conflation [2], but we are concerned only with the text which we may presume Kallimachos knew; we have no reason to believe that the familiar elements were not already welded into this version by Hellenistic times. This story of course involves transparent allegory, for Metis, 'Good Counsel', is no true goddess, as Prof. Rose reminds us [3], being without a cult. Metis stationed inside Zeus serves merely to provide him with an unfailing supply of wisdom. She is installed in Zeus' belly presumably because it is here a seat of knowledge and thought, while Athene is born from Zeus' head perhaps because it contains a great quantity of the stuff of procreation [4]. But Kallimachos extends the allegory. If Metis' physical contact with Zeus' belly inspires his thinking, then Athene's physical contact, in transit, with Zeus' head—through which his omnipotent will is expressed by his nod—may be assumed to have conferred on her not merely 'equal strength and wise

---

[1] Ov. *Met.* 3.336-7.
[2] See, for example, M. W. M. Pope, *A.J.Ph.* 81 (1960), 113 ff.
[3] *Folklore* 1935, 27 f.
[4] For this view see R. B. Onians, *The Origins of European Thought*, etc., p. 233. It is supported by Prof. Pope, *op. cit.* p. 114.

counsel', but also the same effective nod, as an inherited characteristic. Did ever devotee reason like this?

I mentioned earlier that the device is based on the Hesiodic
version of the Teiresias story. Indeed Phlegon (*Mirab.* 4) reports
that Kallimachos also used this version elsewhere. Pfeiffer (ad
fr. 576) is sceptical, for he cannot see a motive for the poet's
use of two versions. Cahen [1] trusts Phlegon, but for the reason
that 'on saisit bien ici comment Callimaque varie la tradition
qu'il rapport suivant le caractère, plus érudit ou plus poétique,
de l'ensemble où elle doit figurer'. I agree with Cahen, but he
has put the cart before the horse. Here the Teiresias story is per-
forming highly specialized service; it would be quite unnatural
to expect it always to be so. If Kallimachos had occasion to refer
to the story again, it would be more likely to be the standard, the
Hesiodic, version.

I hope that by now the framework of ideas which I postulate for
the *Bath of Pallas* has become clear. 'How can I explain away this
savage treatment of Teiresias?', says the poet. 'I shall do it through
a hymn'. The tale requires a Boeotian setting—and presumably
in Pherekydes the divinity was Athene of Alalkomenai [2]—but
Kallimachos exploits the universality of the goddess. What he
says in effect is this: 'I should be using a Boeotian cult of Athene,
but after all Argive Athene is also the goddess of Troy, and there
is no good reason why Athene Oxyderkes should not have a domi-
nion beyond the boundaries of Argos, particularly in the view of
Argive devotees of the goddess, to whom the tale will be addressed.
I need Athene Oxyderkes, because the humane goddess who
sharpened Diomedes' vision may turn Teiresias' pitiful disability
into a glory. She who robbed him of his eyes (and I shall explain
that away by invoking a 'Law of Kronos', which tied her hands, but
not her heart) will justify her cult title by bestowing upon him
penetrating inner vision, the seer's skill.' Was the pattern known
to Nonnos, when he made dying Aktaion say of Teiresias: 'You
have lost the light of your eyes, but you live; and the radiance of
your eyes has Athene transplanted in your mind' (*Dion.* 5. 341-2)?

[1] *Callimaque*, p. 363 n. 1.
[2] See Schwenn, *R.E.* ix A (1934), 131. 30 ff.

CHAPTER THREE

HYMN 5: THE RITUAL FRAME

If Kallimachos is explaining away a crude tale as the central feature of H. 5, we ask what is the function of the elaborate ritual opening. It is, in a sentence, a brilliant manoeuvre designed to prepare us for the savage tale— and then, in retrospect, to show the reader that he has drawn the wrong conclusions from the opening, that the masculinity of Athene prepares us for chivalry as well as martial prowess, for a goddess of proportion as well as power. Kallimachos is never more attractive than in these moments of delightful mischief.

The Structure

There is symmetry in the ritual opening. The first two stanzas are addressed to Athene's bathing attendants, who are excitedly bustled into their positions for the procession. They will meet the statue of the goddess and escort it to the river for its ablutions. And yet not 'it', but 'her', for, as Wilamowitz [1] pointed out, and later writers have corroborated the remark, the images of the goddess's xoanon in its wagon and the goddess herself in her chariot are allowed to blend. It is, already at the beginning, not the statue which has use for olive oil and comb, while at the close of the narrative—in which Athene's humanity has been vindicated—it is clearly the epiphany of the goddess herself that we are to expect. In this regard Kallimachos shows himself an observant witness of the exaggerations of popular devotion. To the Master of Ceremonies above all—but no less to the attendants—the statue is their goddess, and it is, appropriately, in the language of devotion, so prone to extravagance of thought, that the identification is revealed.

---

[1] *Hell. Dicht.* II, p. 15. Cahen (*Comm.*, p. 218 ff.) regards it as significant that there is no mention of the bath of the sacred image in the poem. The reason for the omission I suggest on p. 70. As a result Cahen opposed Wilamowitz' interpretation, concluding that the goddess herself, *coming from Olympos*, is to bathe. But there is no good reason to reject the scholiast's comment on line 1, the less so if we grasp the importance of the 'fluctuating image' in the Callimachean hymn.

In both of the opening stanzas the agitated summoning of the attendants is motivated by dramatic asides: 'I hear the sacred horses whinnying just now. The goddess too is ready to come' (2-3); 'I hear the creak of the axle naves' (14). The device maintains the excited tempo of the opening. Stanzas 3 and 4 bid the goddess process. But within the stanza divisions there is a difference in tempo. In S. 1 the organizer is insistent: ἔξιτε . . . . ἔξιτε . . . . σοῦσθε . . . . σοῦσθε. In S. 2 the procession is forming (ὦ ἴτ' Ἀχαιιάδες, 13, where nothing prevented the poet from writing ἔξιτ', had he wanted to do so); the personnel, trained as one might expect, are responding to his orders. There is time for a somewhat lengthy and academic disquisition on Athene's toilet requirements. In Ss. 3 and 4 the tempo is reversed. In the former, the attendants are ready (πάρα τοι καταθύμιος ἵλα, 33), and Athene is given encouragement to come. The noble clan of the Arestoridai have provided their daughters to serve her, and the Shield of Diomedes will take part, as by ancient appointment. In S. 4 the atmosphere becomes again intense with the insistent warnings of 45-8 and 51-4, for the nearer the arrival of the divinity, the closer the peril of the unwitting male witness.

The Epiphany Hymn

The technique by which the narrator takes part in the ceremony, a mimetic-dramatic technique, has been credited to Kallimachos himself [1], to Theokritos [2], to Sappho [3]. The question is insoluble but, whatever the source of the technique, we can appreciate its power. The manner in which the poet plunges us dramatically *in medias res* confronts us with a spectacle of tense and highly-wrought expectation. We encounter, as it were, an emotional and excited group of devotees celebrating a great festival. The opening recalls Theokritos' *Women at the Adonia*, in which we leave Praxinoa's house to be almost crushed in the crowd and trampled by the processional horses. We are not merely curious bystanders, for the excitement of the movement draws us within the orbit of the action. We may start with the feelings of the unregenerate at a Revival Meeting, but whether those feelings persist will depend on the persuasive oratory of the 'missioner'.

---

[1] C. Pasquali, *Quaestiones Callimacheae* (1913), pp. 148 ff.
[2] L. Deubner, *N.Jbb.* 47 (1921), 376-8.
[3] A. L. Wheeler, *A.J.Ph.* 51 (1930), 218.

Kallimachos preserves the mood of bustle by asyndeton[1] and rapid change of subject. The attendants must process. He hears the sacred horses. The goddess too is ready. The attendants must process. We are to witness an epiphany. On the subject of epiphany hymns Kleinknecht is an eloquent and authoritative guide[2]. He reminds us of the traditional elements which recur in the ritual opening: the technical ἐξιέναι (of the ritual procession, pp. 303-4), the appearance (ἔρχετ' 'Αθαναία, line 137), the reception (δέχεσθε, 137), the acclamation, prayers and ritual cries (139 σὺν τ'εὐαγορίᾳ σὺν τ' εὔγμασι σὺν τ'ὀλολυγαῖς, a felicitous line which, incidentally, seems pitched for the flute)[3], the greeting (χαῖρε, 140, 141). There can be no doubt, from the involvement of the form in half of the poet's hymns, that he found it particularly satisfying and rewarding to introduce this pronouncedly lyrical feature. But that any one of the three hymns may be explained simply as an 'epiphany hymn' —and this is the claim which Kleinknecht makes for H. 5[4]—I strongly doubt.

He would find the epiphany motif carried into the cautionary tale; for example, in the midday *inquiétude* (pp. 328-9), and in the friendship of Athene and Chariklo (p. 327). The latter relationship to him represents the special bond of *theophilia* (cf. line 86), which he connects with φίλοι θεοῦ, an appellation of those who are worthy of a divine epiphany. But such features have a natural place in the story, which, in any case, centres upon, not the appearance of Athene to Teiresias, but just the opposite. At lines 51 ff. the point at issue for the 'cautionary' tale is the sight of the divinity, not her appearance.

[1] Cf. F. L. Shisler, *T.A.P.A.* 73 (1942), 284-5.

[2] Pp. 301-6. Cf. L. Weniger, 'Theophanien, altgriechische Götteradvente', *A.f.RW.* 22 (1923/4), 16-57; F. Pfister, 'Epiphanie', *R.E.* Supp. 4 (1924), 277 ff., esp. 304 f., 314 ff.; H. Kleinknecht, 'Zur Parodie des Gottmenschentums bei Aristophanes [*Aues* 1706-1765]', *A.f.RW.* 34 (1937), 294-313; id., "Die Epiphanie des Demos in Aristophanes' *Rittern* [1316-34]', *Herm.* 74 (1939), 58-65. Kleinknecht's *Die Gebetsparodie in der Antike*, Tübinger Beiträge 28, 1937 is also of use.

[3] Appropriate enough when we remember that the elegiac was originally a flute-song. Cf. van Groningen's comment in *Poésie verbale grecque*, p. 52 n. 1 on Moschos, *Europa*, 98: (φαῖό κεν αὐλοῦ) Μυγδονίου γλυκὺν ἦχον ἀνηπύοντος ἀκούειν. G. Herzog-Hauser, *Wien. Stud.* 64 (1949), 33, saw the sound of the flute in the alternation of *i* and *u*, associated with dentals, in Theocr. 1. 1 ἁδύ τι τὸ ψιθύρισμα καὶ ἁ πίτυς (with an echo in Verg. *Ecl.* 1. 1 Tityre tu patulae). The idea is ably defended by O. Skutsch, *Rh. Mus.* 99 (1956), 200.

[4] Pp. 320 n. 2, 330, 350.

I think rather that Kallimachos shows himself an artist who is prepared to devote as much attention to his frame as to his canvass, for the effect of the picture depends upon a harmonious use of both. The epiphany framework is trimming, but brilliant trimming.

For some of his aids he shows particular affection, especially the stimuli which spur the narrator into excited speech[1]. In H. 5 we have the whinnying horses, the noisy axle. In H. 6 (involving again horses and conveyance), he refrains from mere repetition. The starker emotional content calls for a different image, and so he uses the appearance of the Evening Star. In H. 2—a far more personal document, and in holiday mood (Apollo returns from his winter vacation)—he introduces the laurel, palm and whole temple quivering with excitement, like a faithful hound on his master's return; also the carol of the swan. Kleinknecht[2] compared the description of the epiphany of Hekate in Theocr. 2, 35-6: 'Hark, Thestylis, the dogs are howling in the town. The goddess is at the crossroads. Quick, beat the gong'. The same excitement, the same asyndeton and change of subject; a similar reference to animal reaction to the proximity of the divinity. However I suspect that Kallimachos, drawing upon the same tradition, is giving overtones to casual reference. Just as the midday calm draws its strength from the atmosphere of foreboding with which the hour is invested, so the neighing of the horses becomes, not simply a natural feature of processional organization, but, in relation to the universal appreciation of animal reaction to the uncanny, an indication that an epiphany is near. We begin to wonder whether the horses are restless because they sense the presence of Athene[3].

---

[1] The lyrical *Pannychis* (fr. 227), described by an early summary as a drinking song, opens in a way reminiscent of H. 2: 'Apollo is present in the choir; I hear the lyre. I feel the presence of the Erotes; Aphrodite too is here.' The tone is more subdued, but one notices at least the 'instantaneous aorist' in ἠσθόμην (line 2; cf. ἐσείσατο H. 2.1; ἐπένευσεν H. 2.4; ἐσάκουσα H. 5.3).

[2] P. 303 n. 4. He was anticipated by L. Deubner, *N.Jbb.* 1921, 377.

[3] I am attracted to the interpretation of line 3 given by Kleinknecht, p. 302 n. 2. He points out that it is difficult to bind ἐσάκουσα and ἁ θεὸς εὔτυχος with καί, and so would continue the asyndeton by inserting a colon after ἐσάκουσα, translating καί as 'also', and analysing the thought as 'werden einmal die heiligen Pferde unruhig, dann ist auch die Göttin nicht mehr ferne'. With all this I would agree, but suggest that my idea is a useful supplement, adding a new dimension to the imagery.

Stanza 1: Athene the Charioteer (lines 1-12)

At first sight Stanza 1 seems top-heavy and the treatment laboured, for eight of the twelve lines are devoted to Athene's horses, which may strike us as a non-essential feature. And yet the poet's insistence that Athene never bathed before she had washed her horses, not even when befouled with gore after the Gigantomachy, suggests—as Wilamowitz[1] saw—that a ceremonial washing of the horses preceded the Bath of Pallas (although not necessarily in the river). Furthermore Athene Hippia comes to mind, and in fact Kleinknecht (p. 312) regards the existence of this cult as responsible for the thematic references to Athene's horses in the poem (lines 2-3, 6-9, 44, 61-2, 71, 141-2) [2]. If this is a theme, it is a minor one, one element in a total picture of a *masculine* goddess, militant when aroused, but never *uarium et mutabile*. Although the goddess's masculinity seems to me to be the poet's prime concern, it may be that he is also striking two minor chords. Firstly, that the goddess who thinks always of her horses first (of which every horseman will approve) is a goddess of reason and order. Secondly, in the mention of her as an adversary of 'the lawless Giants', that she is a worker for justice, and no goddess to be trifled with.

In any assessment of Kallimachos' skill we would also do well to notice the verb used for removing the dust from the horses' flanks. It is ἐξελάσαι (6), for the divine charioteer the *mot juste*: χαῖρε καὶ ἐξελάοισα, καὶ ἐς πάλιν αὖτις ἐλάσσαις ἵππως (141-2).

Stanza 2: Athene's Toilet (lines 13-32)

Here the simplicity of Athene's toilet is admirably developed. No perfumes, no alabaster vials—the creaking axle—the theme resumed, no perfumes or alabaster vials, for Athene does not care for concocted ointments. No mirror either, ἀεὶ καλὸν ὄμμα τὸ τήνας —conciliatory words to which I shall return presently. The affirmation of Athene's beauty leads the narrator into a discussion of the Judgment of Paris, the classic clash between Athene, Hera and Aphrodite for the Miss Universe award of Greek mythology [3]. 'Not

[1] *Hell. Dicht.* II, p. 16.
[2] N. Yalouris (*Mus. Helv.* 7 (1950), 65 ff.) has written on the interesting subject of 'Athena als Herrin der Pferde', but I have not seen his article.
[3] I have not forgotten Hera's marriage, but thought it a shame to waste the modern parallel.

even when Paris, the Phrygian, adjudicated at the contest on Mt. Ida did the mighty goddess glance into a copper mirror or the transparent waters of Simois [1], nor Hera either. But Aphrodite took a bronze mirror, and many times adjusted the same curl'. But Athene, straight from a strenuous workout at the racetrack, used only olive oil, and her face shone with a healthy glow.

Now it may seem at first sight a blemish that the poet refers at all to the Judgment of Paris, for Aphrodite's titivation did result in her winning the title; moreover there were some who regarded Athene's rebellion at the verdict as the reason for her role in the Trojan war. At the same time, no one really doubted that it was the bribes which the contestants offered to the judge which really determined the issue [2]. Pallas promised that Paris would lead the Trojans to victory and destroy Greece, Hera that he would rule both Europe and Asia. But already in Homer we are told τὴν δ'ἥνησ', ἥ οἱ πόρε μαχλοσύνην ἀλεγεινήν (*Il.* 24.30) [3]. Paris yielded to Aphrodite's promise of Helen, the most beautiful woman in the world, and thereby of course created the occasion for the Trojan War. It would seem that Kallimachos had such a thought before him, for Paris' judgment and its aftermath were, for Argos, a *felix peccatum*. Without the Trojan War the Palladion and Shield of Diomedes would not have played their present role in Argive religion.

A similar consideration lies behind Kallimachos' brief inclusion of Hera. He is really interested in masculine Athene, but it is effective to introduce the pronounced femininity of Aphrodite as a foil. However, up to a point, Hera duplicates the image of Athene, and could be dispensed with [4]—were she not the principal divinity of

---

[1] Euripides (*Andr.* 284-5; *Hel.* 676; *Iph. Aul.* 182, 1294. Cf. Damocharis, *Anth. Pal.* ix. 633) has the goddesses bathe in a spring before their contest, but Kallimachos does not exploit this feature.

[2] See Eur. *Tro.* 925 ff.

[3] H. J. Rose, *Handbook of Greek Mythology*, p. 107, calls the identification of the tale told by Homer with the story of the Judgment 'quite uncalled for'. V. Magnien (*R.E.G.* 37 (1924), 145-6) has some good remarks to the contrary; he regards the treatment of the sides taken by the three goddesses in the Trojan War (*Il.* 4. 7 ff.; 20. 313 ff.) as evidence of early knowledge of the story. Prof. Rose returns to the subject in *Humanitas* 3 (1950/1), 281 ff., on which see W. Kullmann, *Das Wirken der Götter in der Ilias* (1956), pp. 36 f.

[4] M. C. Waites, *H.S.C.Ph.* 23 (1912), 27, comments on the 'apparent elimination of Hera' at *Athen.* 510c and 687 c, where Athene as *Arete* vs. Aphrodite as *Hedone* is discussed. He even toys with the idea that these two passages 'preserve an older myth than the conventional Judgment of Paris'.

Argos: ἐπεὶ λάχεν Ἴναχον Ἥρη (H. 4. 74; cf. fr. 55.2). Hence her brief but honourable mention.

Meineke seems to have been the first to draw our attention to the poet's source for his opposition of Athene and Aphrodite, the *Krisis*, a satyr-play by Sophokles. It would seem to have been the sequel to his *Eris*, in which the events leading up to the Judgment were treated—the marriage of Peleus and Thetis, the fury of Strife at not being invited, her casting of the apple inscribed 'To the Fairest' [1]. It was presumably the treatment of the theme in the *Kypria* on which Sophokles himself drew [2]. Be that as it may, in the *Krisis*, according to Athenaios (*Deipn.* 15. 687c), Sophokles τὴν μὲν Ἀφροδίτην, ἡδονικήν (ἡδονήν codd., corr. Wilamowitz, *Hell. Dicht.* II, 16-17) τινα οὖσαν δαίμονα, μύρῳ τε ἀλειφομένην παράγει καὶ κατοπτριζομένην, τὴν δ'Ἀθηνᾶν, φρόνησιν οὖσαν καὶ νοῦν ἔτι δ'ἀρετήν, ἐλαίῳ χριομένην καὶ γυμναζομένην.

Here we find not only the precise actions on the part of Aphrodite and Athene which Kallimachos features, but an interesting allegorical motif. Aphrodite is Pleasure, Athene Virtue and Reason. Jebb-Pearson, rightly I believe, have no doubts that the allegory derives from Sophokles, and is not merely an explanatory comment from Athenaios [3]. Our stanza is certainly enriched by the assumption. If read without innuendo being suspected, it is another facet of the masculine image; but if it draws upon a source in which Athene is *Phronesis*, *Nous* and *Arete*, we can see that, here as elsewhere, Kallimachos is really presenting a divinity who may be interpreted as a formidable fighting machine by the unwary reader, when in fact he has safeguarded himself against later complaints that 'we have had one put over us'. He presents Athene equally as a goddess with a proper sense of values and proportion.

Again the masculine image appears, at lines 24-5 and 29-30. It is interesting to notice that the same image is built into the passage on which Kallimachos drew for line 134 (μάτηρ δ'οὔτις ἔτικτε θεάν), namely Aesch. *Eum.* 736 ff., where Athene gives her vote for the acquittal of Orestes:

---

[1] See Jebb-Pearson, *Fragments of Sophocles*, I p. 139.
[2] Kinkel, *Epic. gr. fragm.*, p. 17.
[3] Despite 510 c: ἐγὼ δέ φημι καὶ τὴν τοῦ Πάριδος κρίσιν ὑπὸ τῶν παλαιοτέρων πεποιῆσθαι ἡδονῆς πρὸς ἀρετὴν οὖσαν σύγκρισιν· προκριθείσης γοῦν τῆς Ἀφροδίτης, αὕτη δ' ἐστὶν ἡ ἡδονή, πάντα συνεταράχθη.

μήτηρ γὰρ οὔτις ἐστίν, ἥ μ'ἐγείνατο,
τὸ δ'ἄρσεν αἰνῶ πάντα, πλὴν γάμου τυχεῖν,
ἅπαντι θυμῷ, κάρτα δ'εἰμὶ τοῦ πατρός.[1]

The 'Spartan stars', with whom Athene is compared at 24-5, are the Dioskuroi, Kastor and Polydeukes. At 29-30 Kastor and Herakles are chosen in relation to 'manly olive oil', principally because they are prominent in Doric cult. (It is worth noting that Pindar's Third Olympian, written in a Doric mode, is largely taken up with discussion of Herakles and the Dioskuroi). They are also decidedly masculine types.

This stanza also provides two examples of verbal ambivalence of a kind which the poet enjoys. I shall mention first the one which has no wider significance in the poem. The Dioskuroi are 'Spartan stars'. Why are they 'stars'? One does not expect the word, when predicated of people, to have a literal relevance. *Aster* in the metaphorical sense of 'leading light' must have been a more frequent idea, as at fr. 67.8, where Akontios and Kydippe are καλοὶ νησάων ἀστέρες ἀμφότεροι[2]. But it happens in this case that, as early as Euripides (*Hel.* 138 ff.), there was the tradition that the Dioskuroi were implanted in the firmament. In this case therefore the word is relevant at both levels.

Much more important is line 17, where a direction is given that no mirror be brought for Athene. The reason: ἀεὶ καλὸν ὄμμα τὸ τήνας. This thought has not been handled particularly well by the commentators, which is most unfortunate, for the poet intends it to have an important double role: at its position in the poem it is designed to hint at the darker side of Athene's character, and, in retrospect, to represent the first foreshadowing of the eye complex which dominates the poem. Such a claim will have to be justified, and we may conveniently start with Pfeiffer's indecision *ad loc.* He observes that one manuscript omits ὄμμα τὸ τήνας, while another reads ἔνδυμα τὸ τήνας. The latter inclined him to suspect a *varia lectio* ἔμμα (Et. Mag. εἴματα· ἱμάτια, ἐνδύματα . . . . .

---

[1] Cf. W. F. Otto. *The Homeric Gods* (trans. M. Hadas), pp. 54-5. For the opposition of Masculine and Feminine by reference to olive oil and perfume Kleinknecht compares Xen. *Symp.* 2, 3; cf. also Call. fr. 110. 77-8.

[2] Pfeiffer compares *Il.* 6. 401 for its use in simile, and Eur. *Hipp.* 1123 for the metaphorical use (applied to Hippolytos). It is just worth noting that one version of Hippolytos' death translated him into heaven as the star ἡνίοχος, Paus. 2. 32. 1.

. . . . . Αἰολεῖς, ἔμμα). But 'neque ἔμμα neque ὄμμα placet ('periphra-
sis' pulchritudinis per vocab. ὄμμα ?)'.

Fuller details of the manuscript readings are given by M.T.
Smiley[1], who decided that ἀεὶ καλὸν ἔνδυμα τήνας was the correct
reading. His argument was that ἔνδυμα is rare and hardly likely
to be a scribe's conjecture, and 'it is more apposite than ὄμμα, for a
mirror could not have aided Athene to improve her eye, if it had
been unsightly, whereas it *could* have helped her to rearrange her
dress at need'. It is curious if he looked no further than the few
instances of ἔνδυμα cited by Liddell-Scott[8], for the occurrence of
the word seven times in St. Matthew, once in St. Luke and a dozen
or so times in the Septuagint should have given him pause. Moulton-
Milligan, *Vocabulary of the Greek Testament* s.v. (1919), already
cite a fifth century inscription [2], and Liddell-Scott-Jones now leaves
no room for doubt. The word was not the rarity that Mr. Smiley
imagined. Moreover a reference to clothing is appropriate neither
to its immediate context, nor to the Judgment of Paris episode
which follows. I say this without having in mind the belief, post-
Hellenistic it seems, that the goddesses appeared before Paris
naked. I merely mean that, if Kallimachos had a reference to
clothing here, it is thoroughly lonely.

Pfeiffer is probably right in assigning to a reference to dress
only the status of an alternate reading. Is this much ado about
nothing? So it seems to E. A. Barber[3], who regarded the whole
issue as a storm in a teacup, and translated ὄμμα as 'face'. This is in
fact the way in which it is translated by Mair, Cahen and Howald-
Staiger, with ample justification to be found in Liddell-Scott-Jones.
But it is not quite as simple as that. Ὄμμα means both 'eye' and
'face'. There is no question about which meaning is primary. Now
reference to a mirror does not automatically exclude one meaning;
one could use it to examine both eye and face. Smiley's objection
does not seem to the point, for one can use a mirror to admire
the unchangeable as well as to repair the changeable. In any case,
the poet expressly tells us that there is no call to bring a mirror;
what is 'always fair' may quite naturally be unchangeable. The
reader who settles for 'face' has the comfort of an absence of
reference to eyes in the following lines, but this is, to my mind,

---

[1] *C.Q.* 14 (1920), 64 f.
[2] Dittenberger, *Syll.*[3] 877.
[3] *C.R.* 1954, p. 230.

another case in which two levels of reference are involved. 'Face' is congruous enough, but 'eye' is distinctive. The latter sets in motion a series of connected thoughts.

The poet thinks particularly of 'eye' because he thinks of Athene Oxyderkes. But at this stage the observant reader can apprehend its function only through a more general approach, for the καλὸν ὄμμα of Athene is a known quantity. From the beginning of Greek literature Athene's glance is significant. She is γλαυκῶπις 'Αθήνη [1] (or simply γλαυκή), γοργῶπις (Soph. *Aj*. 450, *Fr*. 844 Jebb-Pearson), ὀβριμοδερκής (Bacchyl. 16.20 Snell). When Athene appeared to Achilles at *Il*. 1. 199, he knew her immediately, δεινὼ δέ οἱ ὄσσε φάανθεν [2]. However the time was to come when Athene's *glaucopia* was regarded as an impediment; *glaukoi ophthalmoi*, whatever shade or combination of grey, green or blue the word conveyed at the time, were out of fashion. And from this time onwards in mythology Athene becomes extremely sensitive to criticism of her eyes.

Let us start with some words of Propertius, who regarded himself as the Roman Kallimachos:

> num sibi collatam doluit Venus? illa peraeque
> prae se formosis inuidiosa dea est.
> an contempta tibi Iunonis templa Pelasgae,
> *Palladis aut oculos ausa negare bonos?* (ii. 28.9-12).

What interests us here is that a denial that Athene has *oculos bonos* is an insult which prompts the goddess to penalize the offender. In Kallimachos we find a conciliatory affirmation that Athene perpetually has a καλὸν ὄμμα. The two statements hang

---

[1] Kuiper, *Studia Callimachea*, II p. 136, makes the identification of καλὸν ὄμμα and γλαυκῶπις, but gives no indication that he understands its function. Kleinknecht (p. 312) grasped the importance of the eye motif, but seems to have believed that the existence of *glaukopis Athene* removes the necessity to give *kalon omma* any specific connexion with Athene Oxyderkes. His fear is that we should otherwise regard the Teiresias story as 'a rare aetiological myth for the cult of Oxyderkes'. As I see it, it is not a question of Teiresias being introduced to account for the cult of Athene Oxyderkes, but of Athene Oxyderkes being introduced to account for the kind of Athene whom the poet portrays in his presentation of the Teiresias story.

[2] E. Watson-Williams (*Greece and Rome* S. 2. i (1954), 38 f.) does not convince me that this clause applies to Achilles, not Athene. Cf. M. Treu, *Von Homer zur Lyrik* (1955), pp. 69 f.

together— to assert that Athene's eyes are fair is to fear the consequences of a statement to the contrary. Hence there is a sinister
touch, in keeping with the martial role of Athene, built into line 17.

There are other passages in which Athene's eyes are mocked.
At 'Hyginus' *fab.* 165.2 Juno and Venus are described as taunting
her when she plays the flute, 'quod . . . caesia erat'. But here Rose
has an interesting comment:

> 'Ipsae ridendae erant si tum primum oculi Mineruae quo colore essent
> intellexerunt. nempe Graecus ita fere scripserat, κατεγέλων τῆς γλωκώπιδος,
> quae male intellexerat Hyginus. ceteri buccas tantum inflatas ridiculas
> uisas tradunt, idque non aliis dis sed ipsi Mineruae.'

Of course one could contend that Athene's *glaucopia* was a
frequent subject for ridicule, utilized on all occasions; Rose's
opening remark would then be discounted. But, in the light of the
absence of this feature of the incident in other authorities, he may be
right in his conclusion. In that case we might find some interest
(but only a little) in the fact that 'Hyginus', however dense, thought
glaucopia a natural subject for jibe.

With Lucian we are on surer, if on later, ground. At *Dial. deor.*
8 he suggests that Athene's helmet was designed to make her
deformity less noticeable. At *Dial. deor.* 20—on the occasion of
the Judgment of Paris, interestingly enough—Aphrodite asks why
Athene does not take off her helmet: ἢ δέδιας μή σοι ἐλέγχηται τὸ
γλαυκὸν τῶν ὀμμάτων ἄνευ τοῦ φοβεροῦ βλεπόμενον; One does begin to
suspect that the time came when, on each occasion that Hera,
Athene and Aphrodite were brought together in literature, verbal
sparring of this sort was in order. It could therefore be that Kallimachos drew upon such an exchange of insults, perhaps even in a
version of the Judgment, which set his mind recalling Sophokles'
Krisis. But we may never know.

To these, the usual examples, D. R. Shackleton Bailey [1] adds
several Roman examples in which eyes like Minerva's are *caesia*
or *flaua*, and on that account unlovely except to the lover. But,
more important, he remarks that since line 11 of the Propertian
passage alludes (as Postgate saw) to an offence of the daughters
of Proitos, it is possible that 9-10 and 12 'also allude to particular
myths, though they may not now be identifiable'. There is in fact
a version of the myth behind line 12 in Anton. Lib. *Met.* 15, pur-
porting to be taken from the first book of Boios' *Ornithogonia*.

---

[1] *Propertiana*, p. 119.

This is a Coan tale of Eumelos, son of Merops, and his three over-
weening and hybristic children, Agron, Byssa and Meropis, who
worshipped only Ge, despising the other divinities. They refused
to attend Hermes' festivals because he was a thief, Artemis' because
she was of nocturnal habits, and Athene's, because she was γλαυκή
θεός and their own eyes were black [1], a much more admired colour.
These three divinities appeared in disguise and encouraged the
offenders to mend their ways, but, meeting only with abuse, they
changed Eumelos and his children into birds. We cannot guarantee
that this version is Hellenistic, but it will at least serve as an
example of the type.

When I argue for a sinister overtone in line 17, it is worth
remembering that both the general γλαυκῶπις and the particular
ὀξυδερκής lend themselves to such an idea. Both readily acquired
a sinister connotation. For γλαυκῶπις some interesting material
is assembled by M. Leumann (*Homerische Wörter*, 1950, pp. 148 ff.);
for the use of δέρκεσθαι and its derivatives see B. Snell (*Discovery
of the Mind*, pp. 2-3) and J. Vendryes (*Choix d'Etudes Linguistiques
et Celtiques*, p. 122). We may start with *oxyderkes*. It needs no proof
that δέρκεσθαι is descriptive of penetrating looks, and is often
best translated as 'stare'. Now the discomfort which we feel in the
twentieth century when we discover that we are being stared at,
in antiquity was sharpened into fear. The stare was a mark of the
Evil Eye. The snake had it, hence he was δράκων, the creature with
the penetrating glance, with the baleful eye. The Telchines had it,
oculos ipso uitiantes omnia uisu [2], and they were γλαυκῶπες καὶ
μελανόφρυες καὶ ὀξυδερκέστατοι [3].

Here it will be noted that both our terms of reference are brought
together. For γλαυκῶπις and the simple γλαυκή (Athene's title at
Eur. *Heracl.* 754 and Theocr. 28. 1) can as readily be interpreted
as 'bright-eyed' as 'grey-eyed'. And if the former, denoting a
characteristic of glance, then a similar development occurs. Snakes
are γλαυκοί at Pind. *Ol.* 8, 37. We would be surprised if this was a
reference to the colour of their skin or eyes. It is far more likely to
refer to an uncanny stare [4]. We may note that the scholiast in

---

[1] The exact reading at this point is quite uncertain, but the point at
issue is clear.

[2] Ov. *Met.* 7.366.

[3] Suetonius περὶ δυσφήμων λέξεων, E. Miller, *Mélanges de litt. gr.*, p. 417.
Cf. Blinkenberg, *Herm.* 50 (1915), 279, 282 n. 1.

[4] See M. Treu, *op. cit.*, p.284.

explanation brings together φοβεροί, φοβερόφθαλμοι and γλαυκῶπες. There is a good defence in Leumann (pp. 149-151) of γλαυκὴ . . . θάλασσα (*Il.* 16.34) as 'das furchtbare, wilde Meer', and of γλαυκιόων (applied to lions at *Il.* 20.172 and Hes. *Scut.* 430) as proceeding from 'den funkelnden oder wilden Blick'.

I cannot pretend that *all* of this is immediately relevant to line 17. But the total picture fortifies the warlike image of Athene and the role of Athene Oxyderkes in the poem. Athene of the penetrating gaze, Athene of the potentially evil eye, Athene who reacts to criticism of her eyes, all of these are associations which present the goddess as a formidable adversary.

STANZA 3: THE SHIELD OF DIOMEDES (lines 33-42)

Of Eumedes we know little more than what the poet tells us:

'And the shield of Diomedes also, Athene, is being brought along, for Eumedes, your favourite priest, taught this custom to the Argives of old. Once when he realised that the people were preparing a scheme to kill him, he fled with your holy image and settled on Mt. Kreion, yes, Mt. Kreion; and you, goddess, he placed on the sheer crags which now bear the name of the Pallatides.'

But that little is precious. For the scholiast tells us that, during the return of the Herakleidai to the Peloponnese, Eumedes was suspected by the Argives (ruled by the House of Orestes) of *wishing to betray the Palladion to the enemy*; alarmed he took the Palladion and went to the mountain called *Ipheion*. The italicised words show that the scholiast is following an independent tradition, and allow us to conclude that Kallimachos is editing his material. Firstly, by suppression of the truth. It stands to reason that no great glory is reflected on either Eumedes or the goddess whom he served—above all in her role as Defender of the City—if the treasonable side of the event is preserved, and so Kallimachos is judiciously discreet.

Secondly, by emendation. The word *Ipheion* is not sufficiently far removed from *Kreion* in form to remove all doubts on the validity of the transmitted text of the scholion, but, as Pfeiffer points out, we do know of an Argive hero called Iphis (Paus. 2.18.5; Apollod. III. 6. 2). A consideration which makes it likely that the scholiast knew what he was talking about is the unlikelihood that the Pallatides had anything to do with Pallas Athene at all. A

recently published Argive inscription [1] disclosed a new *komê*
called Παλλάς, and Charneux pertinently compared Kallimachos'
Pallatides petrai. It seems to me that the poet is tampering with
the facts by introducing a piece of 'popular etymology'. The
tradition involved Mt. Ipheion, but the Pallatides were too useful
to be wasted. Hence he transferred the scene to the mountain on
which the Pallatides were found. As long as there is reason for
regarding *Ipheion* as genuine, we may only draw upon various ancient connections between people called Pallas, people and rivers
called Kreios and Krios, and Athene [2] to the extent of suggesting
that, if Kallimachos knew of them, they would lend his improvement verisimilitude. I suspect that the seemingly inconsequential
and merely stylistic repetition in Κρεῖον δ'εἰς ὄρος . . . Κρεῖον ὄρος
—of a type common enough in both Greek and Latin verse [3]—is not
as innocent as it looks; it is intended to remind the reader of
the change: 'Mt. Kreion, yes, *Mt. Kreion*'. I would therefore dis-
count the suspicion in which some (most recently Trypanis [4])
have held the second *Kreion oros*.

Though we could wish for more knowledge, we have the facts
essential for appreciating the role of the episode in the poet's
scheme. It gives Kallimachos satisfaction to have the opportunity
for an excursion into local history, but in this case it is rendered
necessary by his underlying motif. The amalgamation of the trea-
sures of the cults of Athene Oxyderkes (the shield) and Athene
Akria (the Palladion) for the purposes of this festival—and Kallimachos confers on this union the dignity of a respectable antiquity
(παλαιότερος, 36)—enables him to play upon the associations of
Athene Oxyderkes. At the same time we notice how indirect is the
poet's manner of reference to that cult.

'Ni Théocrite ni ses grands contemporains ne s'efforcent de réaliser des
ensembles solides, d'une composition bien agencée qui superpose des
éléments en une hiérarchie claire et logique. Ils préfèrent les méthodes
subtiles.' [5]

[1] *B.C.H.* 82 (1958), 14 f. At p. 13 it is dated in the 3rd. century.
[2] See Otto Seel, *R.E.* xviii, 3, col. 238. 9 ff.; Radke, *ibid.* col. 245. How
far this involves a genuine connexion of great antiquity (Pallas and Kreios
both being pre-Greek names)—with mythological ordering, as in Kreios as
the father of the Titan Pallas—or ancient manipulation (as in the killing of
the giant Pallas by Athene) is uncertain.
[3] Schneider's edition of Kallimachos, I pp. 338-9; Platnauer, *Latin
Elegiac Verse* (1951), pp. 33 ff.
[4] *J.H.S.* 74 (1954), 203.
[5] B. A. van Groningen, *Mnem.* S. IV. 12 (1959), 24.

Kallimachos leaves it to his readers to draw the proper conclusion as to why the shield is worth one stanza of his introduction.

Moreover the incident is of a type which underlines the awesome nature of the Palladion and the power of the divinity whom it represents. For Eumedes cannily removes the talisman of the city, the image on which the prosperity of the community depends, and, in possession of such bargaining power, succeeds not only in guaranteeing his personal safety, but also in promoting the cult that he serves. At the same time, then, Stanza 3 abets the martial image of Athene and also introduces, through the clue of the shield of Diomedes, a pointer to the role of Athene Oxyderkes.

This is a convenient point at which to take up a deferred topic, the distinctive theory of Kleinknecht (pp. 306-315), that the Argive Palladion and the Shield of Diomedes were one and the same. He leaned heavily upon the wording of the scholion at line 1 τὸ ἄγαλμα τῆς 'Αθηνᾶς καὶ τὸ Διομήδους, rejecting wholeheartedly Meineke's emendation τὸ Διομήδους σάκος. He does so even on the grounds that no good reason is apparent for the scholiast to use σάκος instead of the ἀσπίς of the text; if the scholiast had kept both eyes glued to the text of line 37 we would have lost far more interesting divergences. At the same time Kleinknecht takes his turn in emendation: καὶ το[ῦ] Διομήδους, 'das Agalma, das der Athena und dem (oben im Gedicht genannten und in Argos verehrten) Diomedes zugehört'. Surprisingly (for it would actually have suited his theory), he does not tell us that καὶ τὸ Διομήδους is in fact the reading of Lascaris in the first edition, the manuscripts omitting the τό. It is, to be sure, difficult to decide whether Meineke's correction is warranted, whether καὶ Διομήδους is an intrusion, whether *agalma* has a wider range of meaning than expected, or whether the scholiast is simply wrong. In view of the inadequacy of the scholion at this point, it is also worth remembering that we are at the mercy of the poet for the association of the Palladion and Shield in this procession; *he is devil enough to have invented it to smooth his path.*

It is to Kleinknecht striking that the principal object, the Palladion, is nowhere mentioned by name in the poem, that, on the other hand, the shield of Diomedes is specially mentioned, and explained through the historical item on Eumedes. He quite naturally boggles at the thought that the poet would give a secondary cult object its own *aition* and mention the image of Athene

only in passing. At least it can be said that Kleinknecht is grappling
with a real problem, and that it is to his credit that he rejects at
p. 308 n. 2 both the view of Staehelin [1], that the Eumedes episode
is too short and disturbs the unity of the poem, and that of
E. Diehl [2], that it is a deliberate digression and an illustration of a
personal feature of Kallimachos' style. Kleinknecht sees it as an
essential feature of the poem. But L. Ziehen [3] rightly protested
against his solution to the problem.

In my interpretation the stanza is essential, and in point of
fact there is no dead wood at all in Hs. 5 and 6. The reason why
the shield is named, and the Palladion only indirectly, is that
Athene Oxyderkes is more important for Kallimachos than Athene
Akria. Above all, the Palladion is not highlighted precisely because
at the higher level it is merged with the epiphany of the goddess
herself, at the lower level it is subordinate in imagery to the symbol
of Athene Oxyderkes.

Some have been disturbed by the brevity of this episode, and
have assumed a lacuna covering the restoration of the Palladion
to the citadel, and the actual institution of the rite of Diomedes'
shield. This seems to me quite unnecessary on other grounds than
the poet's preference for allusive reference rather than detailed
comment. It would be easy for a poet to let this stanza get out
of hand. It naturally lends itself to the treatment of a fully developed *aition* in the manner of Kallimachos' large collection. But he
must not forget at this point that he is not telling a story for its
own sake. Moreover in this piece he is using the elegiac couplet in a
special way, not simply as the common medium of narration that it
is in the *Aitia*. This ties his hands severely. He cannot digress with
the colourful asides and dramatic presentation of events that we
find in the *Aitia*, nor can he garnish this type of elegy with the
verbal tinsel appropriate to his brand of narrative elegy. I think that
lines 38-40 teach this lesson better than I can; they hardly rise
above the level of versified prose. With the limitations that the
poet has placed upon him, I am not surprised that he has exercised a
tighter self-control than we could wish. (Of course if it happens

---

[1] *Die Religion des Kallimachos*, Diss. Zürich, 1934, p. 35.
[2] *Der Digressionsstil des Kallimachos*, Abh. d. Herdergesellschaft zu Riga
5, 9 (1937).
[3] 'Das argivische Palladion', *Herm.* 1941, 426-429; cf. *R.E.* xviii, 3 (1949),
175.

that Kallimachos has *invented* the union of Shield and Palladion for the Bath of Pallas, then what I consider artistic reticence is really the product of an historical vacuum, and the poet may laugh at the expense of all of us!)

STANZA 4: THE DANGEROUS DIVINITY (LINES 43-54)

In this stanza a number of strands are gathered together in the first couplet—Athene the charioteer (5 ff., 23), the shield (35), the goddess of power (8, 17), the masculine divinity (29 f.). Athene is presented to us in a thoroughly martial image: 'sacker of cities, wearer of the golden casque, delighting in the clash of horse and shield'. Kleinknecht (p. 314) reminds us that περσέπτολις, 'sacker of cities', recalls the lines of Lamprokles (fr. 1; II p. 123 Diehl), which were wellknown in Aristophanes' day [1]:

Παλλάδα περσέπολιν δεινὰν θεὸν ἐγρεκύδοιμον
ποτικλήζω πολεμαδόκον ἁγνὰν, παῖδα Διὸς μεγάλου δαμάσιππον
ἄιστον παρθένον.

The passage no less recalls the picture of Athene presented by Hesiod at *Theog.* 924-6: 'Bright-eyed Tritogeneia, the terrible stirrer of strife, the queenly, unwearying leader of the host, *who delights in tumults and wars and battles.*' Not surprisingly, the tone of the rest of the stanza is ominous. The narrator, like the raven of Kallimachos' *Hecale*, knows that βαρὺς χόλος αἰὲν 'Αθήνης [2].

Firstly the women are warned. They must use the local springs for drinking, and not the river. The warning is repeated thrice to stress its gravity. The triple warning illustrates not only the usual Callimachean variations upon a theme: βάπτετε . . . πίνετε . . . οἴσετε, but also nice attention to a syntactical fluster, which reflects the agitation of the narrator. An object for βάπτετε must be created from the meaning of ὑδροφόροι. Excitement is expressed in change of verbal idea—drawing, drinking, drawing—as well as in change of subject—watercarriers, Argos, servants. The reason for the need for caution on the part of the women is a simple one: they may sully Athene's bathwater; but the poet presents it with considerable finesse.

---

[1] *Nub.* 967.

[2] Fr. 260. 41 For the special intensity of Athene's antagonism, cf. Alkaios Q1. 3-5 Lobel-Page: Παλλάδος, ἀ θέω(ν | θνάτοι)σι θεοσύλαισι πάντων | (πικροτά)τα μακάρων πέφυκε. The supplements are uncertain, but the sense is clear. See D. Page, *Sappho and Alcaeus* (1955), pp. 283, 285.

καὶ γὰρ δὴ χρυσῷ τε καὶ ἄνθεσιν ὕδατα μείξας
　ἥξεῖ φορβαίων Ἴναχος ἐξ ὀρέων
τἀθάνᾳ τὸ λόετρον ἄγων καλόν.

In my translation I have rendered μείξας as 'covering', rather
than 'mixing', 'blending', for I imagine that the poet was drawing
upon Pind. *Nem.* 4.21: Καδμεῖοί νιν οὐκ ἀέκοντες ἄνθεσι μείγνυον.
No one of course will consider whether in fact the Inachos carries
alluvial gold: gold is the regular adornment of divinity in poetry.
But the idea draws us back to the opulence of Delos in H. 4.260-263,
especially to 263: χρυσῷ δὲ πλήμυρε βαθὺς Ἰνωπὸς ἐλιχθείς, and then
further back to the source utilized on that occasion by Kallimachos,
the Homeric Hymn to Delian Apollo, lines 135 and 139 [1]:

χρυσῷ δ'ἄρα Δῆλος ἅπασα
ἤνθησ', ὡς ὅτε τε ῥίον οὔρεος ἄνθεσιν ὕλης.

Here we have an association of gold, blossoms and mountain peak,
which is probably the source of gold, blossoms and mountains in
H. 5.49-50.

At the same time we notice φορβαίων. Pfeiffer follows Meineke in
doubting its genuineness: 'nomen proprium exspectandum'. Phorbas
comes to mind. He appears in Argive tradition as either the son of
Argos or the father of Arestor, and there is a little evidence for a
connexion of the noun with the second declension, although it is
normally third (*Phorbas*, *Phorbantos*). But then one sobers up, and
asks whether ingenuity is really called for. The reference to vegeta-
tion in the Homeric Hymn would make *phorbaios* reasonable, and
if Greek can say φορβὰς γαῖα (Soph. *Phil.* 700), why not *Phorbaion
oros*? But another reference in Pindar then becomes of interest,
Ol. 2. 72-3, describing the flora of the Isles of the Blest:

ἄνθεμα δὲ χρυσοῦ φλέγει,
τὰ μὲν χερσόθεν ἀπ' ἀγλαῶν δενδρέων,
ὕδωρ δ'ἄλλα φέρβει.

I do not suggest that Kallimachos owes something to this passage;
that assumption would invite us to take his 'gold and flowers' as
hendiadys for 'golden flowers', sadly baroque in so elegant a setting.
But the associations of ideas do show how unobjectionable *phorbaios*
should be.

---

[1] Lines 136-8 being intruded.

While the women are solemnly abjured not to sully Athene's bathwater, at 51-4 the male population is threatened with the consequences of a more dangerous offence: 'Whoever shall see Pallas, Guardian of the City, naked, shall see this Argos for the very last time'. Doubts have been expressed about Kallimachos' wisdom in introducing a warning to men, when in fact the following tale is not addressed to them, but to the waiting attendants [1]. According to my interpretation this is deliberate. The poet, who has introduced the fourth stanza with a martial image of Athene, is inviting us to anticipate that the tale will be a traditional cautionary tale, an aretalogy demonstrating the power of the goddess. That is, that it will tell how Athene *crushed* an offender. We would very much like to know how far he could further this impression through the existence of a belief that the sight of the Palladion was forbidden. Pseudo-Plutarch (*Parall. min.* 17, 309 F), citing Derkyllos (288 F 3 Jacoby), tells of a Trojan named Ilos, who rescued the Palladion when the temple was fired, and was stricken blind for his pains. Since the story invites comparison with Uzzah, it may be an old belief, but we do not know.

At any rate it is a militant Athene whom we expect to see in action. Of course the tale does demonstrate her power, but only after it has demonstrated her humanity. Now such a story, for all its opening as a cautionary tale, would be useless in the role of a thoroughgoing deterrent. It would have been otherwise if the poet had drawn us to conclude from the tale only that not even the son of her especial favourite could escape the penalty of blindness. But he does not stop there, for his primary concern is to justify the nobler attributes of Athene in relation to the savage Pherecydean story. It would therefore have been, contrary to our expectation, a *mistake* to address the tale to the men, for the tenor of the Teiresias story, as Kallimachos remodels it, is out of sympathy with the idea of warning. That it should be told to the attendants is ideal, for it is calculated to increase their admiration for the goddess.

We see therefore that the warning to the men of Argos is a red herring. It maintains the grimness of the opening stanzas, prepares us for a particular sequence of events. But the poet has other ideas. He undermines our appraisal of the situation. Athene, he reminds us, is not merely a formidable warrior goddess, she is also Reason.

[1] Cf. H. Erbse, *Herm.* 83 (1955), 412 f.

The poet's unregenerate audience may no longer invoke Euripides' dictum εἰ θεοί τι δρῶσιν αἰσχρόν, οὐκ εἰσὶν θεοί [1]; the goddess has become a fitting theme for hymnody.

> πολλαὶ μορφαὶ τῶν δαιμονίων,
> πολλὰ δ'ἀέλπτως κραίνουσι θεοί·
> καὶ τὰ δοκηθέντ' οὐκ ἐτελέσθη,
> τῶν δ'ἀδοκήτων πόρον ηὖρε θεός.
> τοιόνδ' ἀπέβη τόδε πρᾶγμα [2].

[1] Fr. 292. 7.
[2] Eur. *Bacch.* 1388 ff.

CHAPTER FOUR

HYMN 5: FORM, METRE AND DIALECT

If Kallimachos has chosen an *Argive* cult as the setting for a *Theban* story because of the associations of Athene Oxyderkes in Argos, as I have tried to show, there is no profit in the assumption that the composition was in any way at all the pendent of an Argive festival. Had a washing rite sufficed, he could have found examples easier to handle; but he needed Athene Oxyderkes. And having decided on Argos, he skilfully ordered all his material to create a harmonious whole. It is easy to overlook how much finesse has gone into the choice of form and dialect and metre. Kleinknecht, for example, discusses metre only in his closing footnote, and dialect never at all.

The Form

There has been a good deal of discussion as to whether one should consider the *Bath of Pallas* a hymn or an elegy. I am sure that the poet would have called it a hymn, an unusual hymn beyond doubt (for the use of the elegiac couplet for such a composition lacks a convincing parallel [1]); but as decidedly a hymn as Philikos' Hymn to Demeter in choriambic hexameters and the anonymous hymn to Demeter composed in alternate epic hexameters and dactylic tetrameters [2].

Having set himself the task of justifying Athene's violent action, he conceived the idea that such a defence would be most natural in the mouth of a devotee of the goddess, who uses the incident specifically to encourage devotion among his audience. This of course will make the poet's task all the harder, but he revels in the challenge. He makes the opening stanzas outwardly conform to the introduction of a cautionary tale; we imagine that we are drawing near to a fearful goddess, a goddess of power, and we expect to be moved to awe by a demonstration of her might.

---

[1] Wünsch, *R.E* ix (1914), 157 ff. and 167, compares the opening lines of Theognis and *Anth. Pal.* vi. 10, xii. 131. Kleinknecht adds the Bacchus hymn in Prop. III. 17.

[2] Page, *Greek Literary Papyri*, no. 91.

Even with the complete volteface which follows, when the story takes such an unexpected turn that awe gives way to admiration, we still move within a natural ritual framework—until the moment when Kallimachos plays fast and loose with the spirit, and divorces the closing *envoi* from any pretence at religious feeling. If this analysis is reasonable, the composition is beyond doubt a hymn.

THE DIALECT

The idea that the Doric of Hs. 5 and 6 was the speech of a particular region was attacked as long ago as 1877 [1]. But Degner's work did not prevent Wilamowitz [2] and Vollgraff [3] from opting for the dialect of Cyrene, nor did it stop V. Magnien [4] from deciding that, although a literary dialect, we are to think of it as peculiarly Syracusan. These are approaches which should be left now undisturbed in the grave which Cahen [5] has dug for them. One real issue, as Legrand [6] saw, was that of dialectal realism, the use of dialect to suit subject or locale.

But at the same time it is a literary use of dialect which is far from pure. Epic elements are preserved when it suits the poet (such as νούσῳ 6.67, Ποσειδάωνα 6.97, ἐείκοσι 6.33). A variety of explanations may account for discrepant dialectal material. For example, ἔπωνε (6.95) would seem to be borrowed from Alkaios, as more expressive in its context than ἔπινε. If we may follow Cahen's suggestion [7], the poet uses the Ionic νηός in the sixth hymn precisely because it has more of a dialectal flavour than the common ναός with its 'Doric' form. Kallimachos also yields to metrical convenience, as with ὁππόταν 5.113, and more than once with non-Doric futures: ἔσσεται, 5.111, the hybrid ἕξομες, 6.125. An examination of the poems actually produces comparatively few Doric forms which have not an epic-Ionic equivalent of the same metrical pattern. This increases our suspicions that the poem, in

---

[1] R. Degner, *De dorismi usu Callimacheo*, Diss. Breslau. I owe knowledge of his conclusions to Legrand, *R.E.A.* 3 (1901), 301 n. 1.

[2] In his edition of Kallimachos, 1907, p. 16.

[3] *Mnem.* 42 (1914), 417; 46, 337. Further references for Cyrene as the dialect will be found in Herter, *R.E.* Suppbd. v (1931), 435. 32 ff. See also C. D. Buck, 'The Dialect of Cyrene', *C.Ph.* 41 (1946), 129-134.

[4] *M.S.L.* 21 (1918-20), 49-85, 112-138.

[5] *Callimaque*, pp. 431 f., 433-443.

[6] *La Poésie Alexandrine* (Payot: Paris, 1924), 116 f.

[7] *Callimaque*, p. 446.

the main, has been mentally transposed into Doric; it is far removed
from the Doric idylls of Theokritos in this regard. Hs. 5 and 6 are
thin gruel when placed alongside the rich dialectal confection which
we possess in *Idyll* 15. The result is that, for Kallimachos' methods
(although not his purpose), we are reminded of the 'Choral dialect'
of Stesichoros and Ibykos, a dialect which was 'largely the Epic
dialect with 'Doric' accents, original ᾱ for Ionic η, and with a
few Doric words and spellings' [1], with the addition, in the case of
Ibykos, of sporadic Aeolisms [2].

Hs. 5 and 6 were not the only occasions on which Kallimachos
wrote in Doric. He used the dialect in his lyrical *Apotheosis of
Arsinoe*, in five of the epigrams (14, 46, 51, 55, 59) and in three
of the Iambi (6, 9, 11). In the thirteenth Iamb he deals with critics
who objected to his writing Ἰαστὶ καὶ Δωριστὶ καὶ τὸ σύμμικτον
(fr. 203.18). Since he was born at Cyrene, there is no doubt that
he would personally have been familiar with spoken Doric, but
his literary Doric is a conventional amalgam. Why does he use
it? In the last century it was fashionable to relate the choice of
dialect to the 'destination' of the Hymns— an Argive festival
for the fifth, a festival of Doric Knidos for the sixth. H. 6, I shall
argue presently, owes its dialect as well as its structure to the
inspiration of H. 5, but for the latter there is no good reason why we
should cease to think of the dialect as dictated by the Doric speech
of Argos, as long as we discard the idea that this feature was in
any way a concession for a racial group for whom the work was
intended. Basically it is a question of a hymn involving Argos, *ergo*
in Doric, of a literary variety. Although we shall have to enlarge
on the literary associations of Doric, it is fundamentally as simple
as that.

THE METRE

Here we encounter the most interesting experiment, for the fifth
hymn alone is written in elegiac couplets. 'The fascination of
elegies', L. P. Wilkinson [3] noted, 'is hard to define. There are
times when we seem to hear them "like Ocean on a western beach":

[1] D. L. Page, *Corinna* (Society for the Promotion of Hellenic Studies
Supp. Paper 6, 1953), p. 81. See pp. 80-83.
[2] This recalls the Doric-Aeolic treatment of *P. Oxy.* I 8, which was cited
in Ch. I.
[3] *Ovid Recalled* (1955), p. 33.

every successive billow gathers in the first four feet of the hexameter, curls over in the dactylic fifth and breaks on the final
spondee, to ebb again with the backwash of the pentameter'. He
goes on to examine other moods besides, but I go no further than
his image of the crash and ebb of a breaker, for it seems to me
best to illustrate the distinct difference in tempo between the
two lines of the couplet. The hexameter is forceful, just right
for heroics; the pentameter is delicate, sinuous, pensive. In the
hands of Archilochos, Solon, Theognis, Xenophanes and others, the
combination of metres became a successful medium for various
kinds of personal verse, satirical, didactic, erotic, reflective and
openly philosophical.

By Hellenistic times, through its use by Mimnermos and Antimachos, it had become a veritable maid-of-all-work. Narrative
elegy, as in Philitas' *Demeter* and Kallimachos' *Aitia*, was a widely
exploited medium. Perhaps we would be surprised if we knew just
how many types of composition were clothed in an elegiac dress
in Hellenistic times. For example, F. Lasserre [1] has recently reminded us that we possess fragments, of Hellenistic date, of the first
elegiac epithalamium that we encounter before the time of Paulinus
of Nola.

However Cahen realized that H. 5, the *Lock of Berenice* and the
Aitia cannot be bundled together simply as elegiacs. H. 5 (and
also the *Epigrams*) show, for example, fewer epic characteristics
in the hexameter. While a spondaeic fifth foot is not offensive
in ordinary elegy [2], the poet refuses it a home in either H. 5 or
the Epigrams. Realization of a distinction within the group of
elegiac poems, curiously, did not stop Cahen from regarding H. 5
as inferior to H. 6 because elegy 'est peu apte au grand lyrisme,

---

[1] *Rh. Mus.* 102 (1959), 222-247, on Pap. Brit. Mus. Inv. 589 (Pack no.
1121). He gives an emended text. This is a poem which, if only it were complete, would merit a lengthy discussion in a work on H. 5. It involves Arsinoe,
presumably the one who married Philadelphos; if so, it is likely to be earlier
than H. 5. The speaker gives a similar series of orders to those in H. 5, involving the purification of Arsinoe's veil and her nuptial bath (ἀγνὰ λοετρά,
cf. H. 5. 113). There is a warning against drinking from the water, and the
conceit that the spring has transformed its muddy, swollen stream for the
occasion. Lasserre (pp. 238-9) would find in the latter feature literary
aesthetics as pointed as H. 2. 108 ff. There is still too much uncertainty over
authorship and contents to allow firm conclusions to be drawn for our hymn.

[2] Examples in the *Aitia* are given by Pfeiffer ad fr. 1. 31. Others occur in
Euphorion fr. 141. 5 Powell; Eratosthenes fr. 22, 35. 9; Philitas fr. 2. 3.
Hermesianax has four in fr. 7 (lines 1, 9, 19, 79).

qui veut de l'étendue et de la liberté d'allure et de souffle' [1]. One would have thought it more profitable to ask whether there is positive gain in the use of the elegiac in the hymn. In fact there is, although the effect is delayed. I imagine that it was not until the first audience or the first readers grasped the tenor of the 'cautionary' tale, that they realized that this was no ordinary use of the elegiac couplet.

The first step was taken by Heinze [2], who saw a connexion between elegiacs and the piteousness of the theme, τὸ ἐλεεινόν. This is undoubtedly true. The soft, flexible pentameter is capable of expressing a tenderness and delicacy that is highly appropriate to the theme. And we are in the presence of a poet who was recognized as having handled the metre with conspicuous success: 'elegiae princeps habetur Callimachus' [3]. At the same time, we may ask whether the harmony between metre and tone which Heinze detects does not require an external criterion, particularly for a metre whose peculiar merits had been affected by its continual overuse. In other words, what is the evidence that Kallimachos' audience would recognize the use as distinctive? From this point of view there is a superior possibility, which explains both dialect and metre together.

D. L. Page has suggested that there was special reason for using such a metre in a composition set in Argos. I recommend to every student of the *Bath of Pallas* his article on *The Elegiacs in Euripides' ANDROMACHE*, published in *Greek Poetry and Life* (Essays Gilbert Murray) [4]. We must proceed to a summary of his argument. Professor Page, in the course of studying the elegiacs of lines 103-116 of the *Andromache*, observed that not only are these the only example of elegiacs in Greek tragedy, but also represent the earliest example of the elegiac *threnos*. And this despite the fact that fifth century authors frequently associate *elegos* with lamentation, and that a view was widespread throughout antiquity that elegy was specifically threnodic in origin. In Pausanias x. 7.4 he found clear evidence that Echembrotos of Arcadia and Sakadas of Argos in the sixth century wrote threnodic elegies, sung to the accompaniment of the flute, and that the officials of the Delphic festival found such

---

[1] *Callimaque*, p. 310; cf. p. 604.
[2] *Ovids Elegische Erzählung*, p. 95 n. 1.
[3] Quint. x. 1, 58.
[4] 1936, pp. 206-230.

works so gloomy and ill-omened that they excluded them from the programme thereafter. There can be no doubt that elegiac threnody was a feature of early Doric poetry, and no obstacle to their having been 'preserved for centuries by the festivals for which they were composed' (p. 230). Page finds in the elegiacs of the *Andromache* the means to strengthen the argument that that play was not presented in Athens, but in fact in Argos [1]. The threnodic elegiacs are then the poet's gimmick for an Argive gallery. Page has nothing in particular to say about Kallimachos, but he realizes that the *Bath of Pallas* continues this same Doric tradition (pp. 217, 218). And so an Argive festival attracts to itself a Doric dialect and a Doric type of elegy.

The subject was taken up again in 1938 by C. M. Bowra [2], when examining the epigram on the fallen of Coronea [3]. To the lament of Andromache and the *Bath of Pallas* he added the epigram of Coronea and also Plato's epigram on Dion's death [4]. He found two new similarities: the address to the object of mourning is made in the second person (cf. 5.87 ff.), and blame or responsibility for disaster is ascribed to divine agency (cf. 5. 81, 85 f.). He concluded that these were features of Doric threnodic elegy.

With so few examples surviving, it is hard to follow the question any further in a positive way, for we run up against the difficulty of distinguishing between features of a special type of composition and elements which are simply germane to threnody of any kind. Page (p. 223 n. 1) presents some parallels between the lament of Andromache and the choral dactylic threnody at Eur. *Supp.* 271 ff. The only one worth mentioning (since tears, supplication and grief are hardly special features) is the embrace: ἐπὶ χεῖρα βαλοῦσα *Supp.* 272 and περὶ χεῖρε βαλοῦσα *Androm.* 115, to which we may

---

[1] I must leave this question to others. Delebecque, *Euripide et la Guerre du Péloponnèse* (1951), pp. 178-202, comes to different conclusions, but I can find no mention of Page's article.

[2] *C.Q.* 32, 80-88 = *Problems in Greek Poetry* (1953), Ch. VI. Cf. the same author in *Oxford Class. Dict.* (1949), pp. 311 f.; A. E. Harvey, *C.Q.* n.s. 5 (1955), 170 f. I know A. Garzya's article on *Androm.* 103-116 in *Giornale Italiano di Filologia* 4 (1951), 354-6 only through *l'Année philologique*, where his view is declared to be that 'Euripides a repris une forme populaire d'élégie qui a son origine dans le monde sacerdotal dorien'. He returns to the subject, I believe, in his edition of the *Andromache* (Naples 1953), pp. 10, 25, 42.

[3] Peek, *Gr. Vers-Inschr.*, I no. 17.

[4] Diehl, *Anth. Lyr. Gr.*[3], I p. 103.

add H. 5.93 ἀμφοτέραισι φίλον περὶ παῖδα λαβοῖσα. We may wonder also whether the type showed a tendency to utilize the tears of the Trojan War; it is natural enough for Andromache's lament, but what of the opening of the epigram on Dion?

Δάκρυα μὲν ᾿Εκάβῃ τε καὶ ᾿Ιλιάδεσσι γυναιξὶ
Μοῖραι ἐπέκλωσαν δὴ τότε γεινομέναις.

Naturally, when so few examples are available, there are scholars who would deny, or at any rate doubt, the existence of the type of composition postulated [1]. If they are prepared to concede that, while there is no Doric threnodic elegy, there are threnodic elegies written in Doric, they may still appreciate the *Bath of Pallas*. But I think that they are wrong. My own contribution will emerge from Chapter VI, in which I shall try to show that Hs. 5 and 6 hang together in the poet's scheme, and that Kallimachos is reviving a particular type of *Doric* composition in both; that at H. 6.7 ff. the function of Demeter and Hesperos points to H. 5 as a threnodic composition. If I am right, the poet himself answers our questions.

The Endymatia

The great unknown, which he does not answer, is whether in fact we are dealing not simply with a Doric threnodic elegy which is as appropriate to Argos as to any state in the Peloponnese, but rather with a type specifically associated with the Bath of Pallas. A little information on early musical festivals is provided by Pseudo-Plutarch, *Mus.* 9 (*Mor.* 1134). He connects Terpandros with their first institution in Sparta, later followed by Thaletas of Gortyn, Xenodamos of Cythera, Xenokritos of Lokris, Polymnestos of Kolophon and *Sakadas of Argos*:

Τούτων γὰρ εἰσηγησαμένων τὰ περὶ τὰς Γυμνοπαιδίας τὰς ἐν Λακεδαίμονι λέγεται κατασταθῆναι, τὰ περὶ τὰς ᾿Αποδείξεις τὰς ἐν ᾿Αρκαδίᾳ, τῶν τε ἐν ῎Αργει τὰ ᾿Ενδυμάτια καλούμενα.

About the *Endymatia* of Argos we know nothing, but the title, with its reference to clothing (*enduma*) is intriguing. Wilamowitz went so far as to identify the festival with the Bath of Pallas:

---

[1] E.g. P. Friedländer-H. B. Hoffleit, *Epigrammata*, p. 66 n. 5; H. Lloyd-Jones, *J.H.S.* 1955, p. 158.

'Wie in Athen musste das Bild auch ein neues Kleid erhalten; daher hiess das Fest ἐνδυμάτια, Ps. Plutarch Musik 9, die Waescherinnen aber γεραράδες αἱ τὸ τῆς ᾽Αθηνᾶς ἐν ῎Αργει ἄγαλμα ἐνδύουσαι, Bekk. An. 231. ¹'

It pays to keep one's head over this exciting identification, for it remains pure conjecture. If it is right, it may explain more than why Kallimachos has used threnodic elegy in relationship with the *Bath of Pallas*; it may also account for the variant ἔνδυμα (or ἔμμα) at line 17. Unfortunately, it would still be obscure whether it represented an intelligent scribal guess or a reading deriving from Kallimachos. There are considerations which incline me to disregard, however, reluctantly, Wilamowitz' suggestion, in the present state of our knowledge.

In line 17 ὄμμα as 'eye' has relevance for the poet's use of Athene Oxyderkes; as 'face' it introduces the Judgment of Paris scene, in which no mention is made of clothing at all. If Kallimachos were making an oblique reference to the name of the festival involved, it would be a reference which adds nothing to the imagery of the composition, and Hs. 5 and 6 are unique for their freedom from merely *frivolous* obscurity.

For the festival itself, we cannot be completely confident that in fact provision of a new robe goes hand in hand with a ritual bath. Of course it seems natural when one starts with thoughts of the ritual bath, but it is equally possible to imagine an annual clothing of a goddess as a separate ceremony. Or, when mention is made of the Attic Plynteria, there is another complication. There a washing of Athene's robe was certainly involved, but the ritual bath of Athene herself at Phaleron, *as part of the same festival*, is by no means as well established ². It may well have been a separate ceremony.

DIALECTAL SONORITY

When I suggest that it was under the influence of the Argive locale of the Bath of Pallas that Kallimachos used the Doric dialect,

---

¹ *Hell.Dicht.*, II p. 14. Cf. I pp. 182 f. Kleinknecht refers to comments by Wilamowitz in S-B. Berlin 1921, p. 951 n. 4, which I have not seen.

² See, for a good summary of the evidence, C. J. Herington, *Athena Parthenos and Athena Polias* (Manchester Univ. Press 1955), p. 30 and n. 2. Cf. also Farnell, *Cults of the Greek States* I, p. 262; Ziehen, *R.E.* xxi, 1 (1951), 1061. 7 ff. For the offering of the Peplos every four years at the Greater Panathenaia, see Herington, pp. 32 ff.; for offerings of clothes as a common practice, W. H. D. Rouse, *Greek Votive Offerings* (1902), pp. 274-7. Hera received a new *peplos* at Argos every four years (Paus. v. 16, 2; Deubner, *Attische Feste*, p. 30); must we assume a ritual bath of the divinity to boot? At Nauplia Hera bathed annually (Paus. ii. 38, 2).

I have not forgotten an excellent comment of Prof. B. A. van Groningen [1]. He asks why Hellenistic poets were so fond of utilizing Ionic, Doric, Aeolic and dialectal mixtures. 'Partly, obviously, from a simple desire for originality. Partly also because they like *jeux d'esprit* and want to display their learning. But there is another factor which is persistently ignored. It is verbal sonority.' I have deferred the discussion of this subject until now because, in the case of the *Bath of Pallas*, it is only part of the answer. It shows the use that the poet makes of Doric, rather than the reason for his use of Doric at all.

If early Dorians had made a feature of threnodic elegy, one contributing factor was assuredly that the speech lent itself to threnody. Not, of course, that any Dorian felt his speech to be noticeably lugubrious—we have only to think of the magic of Theocr. 1. 1 ff. But it was capable of effects which would seem to him right for it, and to a speaker of, say, Attic-Ionic eminently so. The first feature which comes to mind is the retention of long alpha, by no means peculiar to Doric, but a characteristic whose effect was clearly appreciated in the choral sections of tragedy (whatever its origin there). It is worth noting that, if, as Page suggests, the elegiacs of the *Andromache* are a concession to an Argive audience, the retention of long alpha is still the only dialectal feature which the lines contain. In fourteen lines there are 26 examples of it, almost two a line.

To the grammarians [2] alpha was the most euphonious of the long vowels. As a class we may distrust them, but in the hands of a skilful poet long alpha was used for special effects which the grammarians would find difficult to ignore. We are concerned with only one effect, the striking of a plaintive note. It is worth recalling the form in which the broad character of Doric is the subject of non-Dorian indignation at Theokritos *Id.* 15.87-8:

παύσασθ᾽, ὦ δύστανοι, ἀνάνυτα κωτίλλοισαι,
τρυγόνες. ἐκκναισεῦντι πλατειάσδοισαι ἄπαντα.

Turtle-doves are, beyond doubt, proverbial chatterers, but it is also to the point that at *Id.* 7.141 their sound is a moan, ἔστενε τρυγών [3].

---

[1] *Poésie verbale grecque*, pp. 28 f.
[2] See W. B. Stanford, 'Greek Views on Euphony', *Hermathena* 61 (1943), 3-20, esp. p. 7.
[3] Cf. Verg. *Ecl.* 1. 58: gemere . . turtur.

Now H. 5, of 142 lines, contains either 178 or 179 long alphas (γέρα in 120 being of uncertain length). These include fourteen cases of Dor. α = Att. ω (e.g. πρᾶτον, τᾶν ἱερᾶν ἵππων), which were denied to Euripides. The poem is ten times longer than the elegiacs of the *Andromache*, and so it is not surprising that the latter shows a higher percentage of long alphas per line. But what is noteworthy is that, in total effect, Kallimachos is just as successful. For a second characteristic of Doric was the appearance of omega in cases where Attic-Ionic showed ου (such as ποταμῶ, 46).

By exploiting this characteristic Kallimachos introduces 138-140 omegas into the poem. (I take ὑπαξονίων/ὑπαξόνιον, 14 and παλαιοτέρως/παλαιότερον, 36 as disputed readings.) Kallimachos intends us to take long alpha and omega together in appreciating the total effect. The *Andromache* elegiacs contain 9 omegas and 26 long alphas, a total of 2.5 per line. Over ten times the length Kallimachos achieves 2.2 per line. In this regard there is an impressive evenness between the 62 lines of the framework (143-145 examples, averaging 2.3 per line) and the 80 lines of the tale (173-4 examples, averaging 2.16).

That the ancients used omega for sonorous effect really does not require proof. The verses which Homer [1] was made to quote, during his Agon with Hesiod, include, in a graphic description of battle, three lines which feature no fewer than seven genitives plural (*Il.* 13.341-3); by way of contrast, at *Od.* 4.442 omegas help to reproduce the rich reek of the seals: φωκάων ἁλιοτρεφέων ὀλοώτατος ὀδμή. Hesiod also shows a fine effect in his wellknown Πληιάδων Ἀτλαγενέων ἐπιτελλομενάων (*Works and Days* 383), enthusiastically proclaimed by F. L. Lucas [2] 'a roll of religious music, a line for which Marlowe would have given his ears, a peal of thunder beyond the compass of our tamer tongue'. At the other end of the scale we note the Hesiodic parody in Schol. Ar. *Pax* 1001 [3]: ἀρχομένων σικύων καὶ ληγουσῶν κολοκυνθῶν. The mock-didactic tone we may perhaps capture in 'During the cucumber's advent and passing parade of the pumpkin', but reproducing the sonority is another matter.

In archaic genitives plural in -άων ᾱ and ō support one another;

---

[1] For Homeric usage see Shewan, *C. Ph.* 20 (1925), 206; Stanford ad *Od.* 9. 415-6.
[2] *Studies French and English* (1934), p. 66.
[3] Strömberg, *Greek Proverbs*, p. 94.

similarly in Kallimachos. For example, they underline the clash of battle (44):

ἵππων καὶ σακέων ἀδομένα πατάγῳ
(–ō | –◡◡ | ó̆ || ắ ◡◡ | ắ ◡◡ | ó̆)

Or the emotion of Athene at 79 (to be discussed in Ch. V):

–◡◡ | ó̆ ◡◡ | ắ ◡◡ | ó̆ ◡◡ | ắ ◡◡ | ắā

Or Teiresias' physical pain (84): ó̆ ◡◡ | –ō | ắ || –◡◡ | ắ ◡◡ | ắ, immediately followed by Chariklo's mental agony (85): ắ– | ắ◡◡ | ắ◡... On occasion the sequence of accented vowels is internal, as in the awed tones of 65, at the disclosure of the extent of divine favouritism:

–◡◡ | ắ– | ó̆ ◡◡ | ó̆ ◡◡ | ắ ◡◡ | –ō

Throughout the poem the poet carefully organizes his alphas and omegas to create a general plaintive effect. In their Doric forms, for example, Athene and Demeter seem perpetually wedded to grief. Aktaion's youth is tinged with pathos by the word itself, *habatan* (109). Μάτηρ and κῶρος also play their part. But the effect is as evident in key thoughts as in keywords. The scene of the crime involves a skilful use: the spring (ō-ā-ā-ō-ā-ā, 71), the midday calm (ō-ā-ā-ā, 72), the deep calm (ā-ā-ā, 73). If it were not the sinister hour of midday it would still be difficult, because of the vocalism, to escape the foreshadowing of Teiresias' doom. Compare in the sixth hymn the first onslaught on the sacred poplar (39): ἀ πράτα πλαγεῖσα; we are invited to hear the crash of the axe.

The use that Kallimachos makes of the long vowels is particularly apparent in the pentameters, in which there was always a tendency in Greek towards two rhyming cola. Of the 71 pentameters 6 show a rhyme in ā, ten a rhyme in ō, five show ..ā / ..ō and five ..ō / ...ā. That is, 37 % have ā and / or ō in these positions. In another 26 cases ā or ō appears at the end of one colon. In other words, 73 % of the pentameters contain ā or ō in at least one position, and 37 % have them in both. The curious thing is that Kallimachos is not extending himself in this regard. If fragment 75, the Akontios and Kydippe episode, which contains 37 complete pentameters were rendered into this kind of Doric, 43 % of pentameters would feature ..ō / ..ō, ..ā / ..ā, ..ā / ..ō or .. ō / .. ā while 70 % would show ā or ō in at least one position.

Appreciation of the sonority of the long vowels is not a Calli-machean preserve. In Philitas fr. 10 it is eta and omega which work together:

> οὔ μέ τις ἐξ ὀρέων ἀποφώλιος ἀγροιώτης
> αἱρήσει κλήθρην, αἱρόμενος μακέλην.

And Aratos' cawing crow has often been admired:

> ὥρη ἐν ἑσπερίη κρώξῃ πολύφωνα κορώνη (1002).

But more pertinent is Theocr. 15. 87, which was quoted earlier in this chapter. There the indignation of the speaker appears in - - | ό - | ἄ ◡◡ | ἄ ◡◡ | ό - | - -. Admittedly, one has to be careful in quoting Theokritos. He is not intent on producing patterns of sounds with the same purpose as Kallimachos. He has a fine ear for sonority, but his effects are not necessarily always emotive, or even intentio-nal. We observe the same fact in Homer. Ἐξ Ἐνετῶν ὅθεν ἡμιόνων γένος ἀγροτεράων (*Il.* 2. 852) happens to reproduce both the sonority and the triple rhyme of Hesiod's famous line, yet it has no special character at all. The formulaic nature of the epic and its broad canvass made it difficult for the poet to husband sound effects. In Theokritos it is the Doric which produces the same effect, for the dialect is naturally broad. For example, *Id.* 6. 2 (τὰν ἀγέλαν πόκ' Ἄρατε συνάγαγον), despite the fall of the ictus on four long alphas in succession, is not emotive—but it is none the less deliberate, designed, I think, to sustain the effect of the use of dialect. That is, the repetition of the vowel impresses upon us the dialectal setting.

But there is feigned grief at 10.40 ὤμοι τῶ πώγωνος, ὃν ἀλιθίως ἀνέφυσα (ό - | ό ō | ό ◡◡ | ἄ ◡◡ / ό ◡◡ | -◡, and O. Skutsch [1] has suggested that at 1. 115 Theokritos goes out of his way to increase the sonority of the line by introducing the rare φωλάδες to provide a sixth omega: ὦ λύκοι, ὦ θῶες, ὦ ἀν' ὤρεα φωλάδες ἄρκτοι,/χαίρεθ'. The effect here can reasonably be regarded as underlining the sense of sorrowful farewell.

Into which category should *Id.* 7. 155 be placed? It would be hard to surpass for sheer sonority:

> βωμῷ πὰρ Δάματρος ἀλωίδος; ἇς ἐπὶ σωρῷ
> (ό ō | - ā | ἄ ◡◡ | ό ◡◡ | ἄ ◡◡ | όō).

Since the context of 154 and 156 provides the body of the thought,

---

[1] *Rh. Mus.* 99 (1956), 200.

and 155 contains only syntactical odds and ends, one could be sceptical about the thought that the line serves any purpose through its sonority. But I doubt whether a Hellenist could create such phonetic symmetry without ulterior motive. I should prefer to think that the syntactically delayed sonority of βωμῷ πὰρ Δάματρος ἀλωίδος suddenly intensifies the fervour of Theokritos' memory of the draught described in 154, that, in conjunction with it, ἇς ἐπὶ σωρῷ intensifies the solemnity of the prayer of 156. Theokritos strikes a chord which reverberates throughout the passage.

In Kallimachos it is predominantly long alpha and omega which give the use of dialect special effect. The only consonantal change of any note is Doric k = Attic t (e.g. ποκά = ποτέ, 57). While there are only eight examples in the poem, palatal alliteration is marked, giving a crispness to the tone, and four of the eight cases are involved (5, 18, 59, 67—six palatals in the last reference). Other examples are to be found in lines 28, 30-32, 40, 71, 83-4, 91, 103, 139-140. Line 30 is particularly effective:

ᾧ Κάστωρ, ᾧ καὶ χρίεται 'Ηρακλέης.

Kleinknecht (p. 322 n. 2) compared Prop. II. 1, 25 and IV. 11, 21 as other examples of the use of one member of a pair to refer to both (just as here mention of Kastor does not exclude Polydeukes). However Kastor is principally chosen because he has phonetic advantage over his twin. Notice also line 40, in which omega and palatals cooperate: ᾤχετ' ἔχων Κρεῖον δ' εἰς ὄρος ᾠκίσατο.

This then is what Doric essentially means to Kallimachos for this type of composition—the deployment of long alphas and omegas and palatal alliteration to create a heaviness which we are to construe as plaintive. The reader can discover minor effects for himself. I do not mention them here, because I do not wish to obscure the fundamentally narrow range of the poet's major dialectal effects. We shall see in Ch. VI that, when he wishes to recreate the atmosphere of H. 5 at the beginning of his later hymn, it is to the effect of alpha, omega and palatal alliteration that he returns; when his purpose has been served, the effects fall noticeably away. When we recall how exacting were the demands of stagecraft for the poet's purpose in H. 5, we shall not be surprised that dialectal effects are so few; but, if we are honest, we shall acknowledge their success.

The effect of sound is a personal experience. It does not affect us all in the same way and often resists analysis. But the teacher is not worth his salt if he does not try to communicate impressions, however lame his language, however feeble the example may appear to some. I shall essay a comment upon two lines which have left an impression upon me.

μάτηρ μὲν γοερᾶν οἶτον ἀηδονίδων
ἆγε βαρὺ κλαίοισα, . . . (94-5)

It is, oddly enough, the last three words which I want to discuss. Their effect seems to me similar to one which I described in *Symbolae Osloenses* 1960, 18 f., and it is to the point to allude to it again here. Twice in the Odyssey Homer uses a rare collateral form of *aeido*, *aoidiao*. It occurs in related scenes, those of Kalypso and Kirke:

Od. 5. 61-2:   ἡ δ'ἔνδον ἀοιδιάουσ' ὀπὶ καλῇ
              ἱστὸν ἐποιχομένη χρυσείῃ κερκίδ' ὕφαινεν·
10. 226-7:   Ὦ φίλοι, ἔνδον γάρ τις ἐποιχομένη μέγαν ἱστόν
              καλὸν ἀοιδιάει.

Stanford very pertinently observed that the number and variety of vowels 'fill the word with melody'; with very little exercise of the imagination we can actually hear the ladies singing as they weave. In Hesiod's fable of the Hawk and the Nightingale (*Works and Days*, 208), the arrogant hawk tells the helpless nightingale that she must go wherever she is taken, for all her being a song-stress: τῇ δ'εἷς, ᾗ σ'ἂν ἐγώ περ ἄγω καὶ ἀοιδὸν ἐοῦσαν. In the reiterated vowels (ηι-εις-ησ: εγω-αγω) and sonority of the first part of the line I believe that I hear the staccato screech of the hawk, and in καὶ ἀοιδὸν ἐοῦσαν an identical effect to that which Homer creates by *aoidiaein*. That is to say, in its effect καὶ ἀοιδὸν ἐοῦσαν is no different from καὶ ἀοιδιάουσαν. The aggressor ironically reproduces the melody of his victim. Homer's usage involves literary artifice, while Hesiod uses the melody built into Greek itself.

Similarly, I am tempted to believe, Kallimachos, when alluding to the nightingale, also echoes the bird's powers of modulation. The powers which Pliny mentions in the locus classicus on the nightingale (*Nat. Hist.* X. 43): 'Tanta uox tam paruo in corpusculo, tam pertinax spiritus . . . in una perfecta musicae scientia modulatus editur sonus'. Of course there is no single way of achieving such an effect. It is open to every careful and sensitive craftsman who watches the way in which his vowels are juxtaposed; there is a level at which the effect may be unconscious. But it should, I think, make us alive to the possibility that, with a clever author, dissimilarity in vocalism *may* be as intentional and as striking as repetitive features.

My second illustration is likely to gain a more kindly reception: συρίγγων ἀίω φθόγγον ὑπαξονίων (14) [1]. I would call it the happiest line in Kallimachos. Now it is interesting to find that Greek poets were as sensitive to the music of carts and chariots as we are to the roar of an express train or the chug of a steam engine. This is hardly surprising in the days before rubber tyres and macadamized roads, but I am still impressed by the number of occasions on which the effect is reproduced in poetry. They are worth a paragraph.

At Hesiod *Works and Days* 692-3 we hear the strained and breaking axle: δεινὸν δ', εἴ κ' ἐπ' ἄμαξαν ὑπέρβιον ἄχθος ἀείρας/ἄξονα καυάξαις καὶ φορτία μαυρωθείη: ...ák...ák...ák...kaúak [2]; it breaks again in Kallimachos' *Hecale* (fr. 260.53): ἄξονα καυάξαντες. Already in Homer its creak is heard as Athene boards Diomedes' chariot at *Il.* 5. 838: μέγα δ'ἔβραχε φήγινος ἄξων/βριθοσύνῃ, and again at Aesch. *Sept.* 153: ἔλακον ἀξόνων βριθομένων χνόαι. In the latter a more complicated pattern starts to emerge, for the repetitive feature (ak ... ak) is combined with *i, o* and the harsh *chn*. We owe it to E. Moutsopoulos [3] that the artful chariot music in this poet has been brought to notice, especially the sequences of *Suppl.* 181: σύριγγες οὐ σιγῶσιν ἀξονήλατοι and *Sept.* 203-5: ἔδεισ' ἀκού/σασα τὸν ἁρματόκτυπον ὄτοβον ὄτοβον/ὅ τι τε σύριγγες ἔκλαγξαν ἐλίτροχοι. Kallimachos is as sensitive to the music: ἄξων/τετριγὼς ὑπ' ἄμαξαν (fr. 260.67-8), and also Leonidas of Tarentum (*Anth. Pal.* vii. 478.3-4):

> μνῆμα δὲ καὶ τάφος αἰὲν ἀμαξεύοντος ὁδίτεω
> ἄξονι καὶ τροχιῇ λιτὰ παραξέεται.

The charm of our line is the charm of Aesch. *Suppl.* 181 and *Sept.* 203-5; there is a complicated pattern of discordant sounds. We see the whole line as one phase of a movement which goes on

---

[1] Editors are sharply divided on the reading of the final word. EQS read ὑπαξόνιον, the others ὑπαξονίων. It would seem that the archetype offered a choice (Smiley, C. Q. 14, 1920, 121). I make my choice on the basis of sound.

[2] See further *Symb. Osl.* 35 (1960), p. 19.

[3] *R.E.G.* 72 (1959), 52.

repeating itself. A combination—if further analysis is not irreverent — of strident, booming, resonant, metallic sound, an attempt at orchestration. And, more impressive still, the poet has worked this lyrical effect into the pentameter. Whatever the limitations of Kallimachos—to which I must now turn—his sensitivity to sound cannot be denied.

CHAPTER FIVE

HYMN 5: FORM AND FEELING

Technical mastery over his material we cannot deny to the poet, but what of the emotional content of his poetry? On this subject there is a widely held and traditional verdict: Kallimachos is cold, unfeeling, ironically aloof from both the maudlin and magnificent in emotional display, to avert a general charge of sentimentality. This verdict seems to me fundamentally correct. But Ernst Howald, in his sensitive aesthetic study, *Der Dichter Kallimachos von Kyrene* (Zürich 1943), and in the Howald-Staiger edition of the poet (1955), combats the traditional view. He appropriates a phrase from *Epigr.* 44.2, properly descriptive of smouldering love, and declares it a useful summary of Kallimachos' own nature: πῦρ ὑπὸ τῇ σποδιῇ, 'unter der Asche ein Glühn', 'a flame under the ashes'. To Howald he is above all the 'passionate' poet, *leidenschaftlich*. I only wish that I could agree.

Howald would find 'a flame under the ashes' in the celebrated second epigram, on the death of Herakleitos [1]. It is worth citing, especially for the English speaker, who, hypnotized by Cory's translation, can easily forget that there is a Greek original with effects of its own.

> Εἶπέ τις, Ἡράκλειτε, τεὸν μόρον, ἐς δέ με δάκρυ
> ἤγαγεν· ἐμνήσθην δ' ὁσσάκις ἀμφότεροι
> ἥλιον ἐν λέσχῃ κατεδύσαμεν. ἀλλὰ σὺ μέν που,
> ξεῖν' Ἁλικαρνησεῦ, τετράπαλαι σποδιή,
> αἱ δὲ τεαὶ ζώουσιν ἀηδόνες, ᾗσιν ὁ πάντων
> ἁρπακτὴς Ἀίδης οὐκ ἐπὶ χεῖρα βαλεῖ.

The high respect in which this epigram is held is fully justified. The way in which thoughts spill over their barriers in the first four lines, the magic of κατεδύσαμεν (suggestive of a communion of uncommon power), the skilful location of key thoughts (τεὸν μόρον, κατεδύσαμεν, ἀηδόνες) [2], the pathos of an unknown grave and

---

[1] *Der Dichter*, pp. 63 f.
[2] For the artistic use which Kallimachos makes of the space between the caesura in the third foot and the bucolic diaeresis at the end of the fourth,

an abiding grief cannot but move us. Above all, the suggestion of unfathomable sorrow. But Howald himself [1] notes that Kallimachos personally is involved in few of this kind of epigram. And, after all, we expect personalities exposed to violent opposition to value friendships highly. If, then, the poet shows emotion over the memory of a cherished friendship, it can hardly stamp him as exceptional, any more than it can be used by those who support the traditional view to accuse him of being unfaithful to the movement's aversion from sentiment.

What of epigrams which tell of another's sorrow? Epigram 19 Pfeiffer (21 Schn.) shows that Kallimachos can produce at second hand the quiet, brooding restraint that speaks of deep grief in the best of Classical sepulchral epigrams:

Δωδεκέτη τὸν παῖδα πατὴρ ἀπέθηκε Φίλιππος
ἐνθάδε, τὴν πολλὴν ἐλπίδα, Νικοτέλην [2].

But neither will such as this advance us on our way. We must remember that the type was inevitably seldom composed by the bereaved. Doubtless the best of its Classical exponents had an ability to identify themselves with the mourners, or at any rate share their sorrow. But, in Hellenistic practice, the type could call forth no more than the ability to create a convincing illusion, the more so as it is the apparently untapped store of emotion on which the mourner draws, rather than the amount which he expressly exhibits, that gives the type its power. Such restraint made the type ideal for poets who shrank from displays of uninhibited emotion. It was not impossible to paint a brilliant picture of the still waters of grief, and leave to others the conclusion that they ran deep:

σοὶ μὲν δοκεῖν ταῦτ' ἔστ', ἐμοὶ δ'ἄγαν φρονεῖν. [3]

I do not wish to be misunderstood. In this chapter I am not denying that Kallimachos may have been of passionate tempera-

---

there are some valuable remarks by J. Carrière, 'L'effet de double coupe dans l'hexamètre de Callimaque', *Pallas* (Annales publiées par la Faculté des Lettres de Toulouse), 5 (1957), 5-15 (p. 10 for *Epigr.* 2).

[1] Howald-Staiger, p. 171.

[2] For an analysis of this couplet see B. A. van Groningen, *Poésie verbale grecque*, pp. 72 f.

[3] Soph. *Aj.* 942. For a good paragraph on the contrast between Hellenistic reserve and Classical exuberance in emotional display see Van Groningen, *Mnem.* S. IV. xi (1958), 304.

ment. What I am denying is that we have a right to find it reflected
in his poetry. The principles of the movement stood in his way.

Howald would find passion above all in the epiphany hymns, in
which beyond doubt the poet shows an admirable skill in depicting
emotion. 'The piety is not real, but the feeling is real' [1]. This I
grant. But he would go further [2]. The poems testify to a tense
and hopeless conflict between Kallimachos' welling emotions and
the cold manner of his narrative art. He 'capitulates', especially
in the myths introduced; the manner 'triumphs'. Only in H. 2 is
the emotion in any way sustained. We even read of the 'subterra-
nean and almost demoniac passion of the later hymns' [3]. It is
obvious that my interpretation of H. 5 allows no place for this
conflict. Where emotion is generated, what is there to suggest that
it is not a cold-blooded academic analysis of feeling, no different
from the rest of his intellectual activity? That Kallimachos could
feel what he was describing still has to be proved.

A strong argument against it is the way in which Howald over-
plays his hand. For example, an analysis of the feelings inspired
by H. 6. 25 ff. starts in this way [4]:

> 'The solemn picture of Demeter's sacred grove with its calm and un-
> disturbed character, often chosen by the goddess for her place of residence,
> makes us uneasy and anxious. We feel the approaching calamity and
> wince as the twenty giant servants come rushing along with their young,
> blinded leader at their head. We feel that the catastrophe is unpreventable.'

Now a glance at the text will sober us up. Kallimachos is not
Ovid, depicting the eeriness of a 'silua uetus . . nulla uiolata securi':

> stat uetus et multos incaedua silua per annos:
>   credibile est illi numen inesse loco.

There is nothing mysterious about peartrees, nothing uncanny
about sweetapples. The poet in fact says *nothing* to suggest 'Stille
und Unberührtheit'. Nor are there even undertones of unrest. If
to some the character of Demeter's grove recalls the gardens of
Alkinoos (*Od.* 7.114 ff.) and Kalypso (*Od.* 5.238 ff.), both unearthly
creatures, we need go no further than Theokritos *Idyll* 7.135 ff.,
to find the worship of Demeter celebrated in an everyday scene
among a remarkably similar variety of trees.

---

[1] Howald-Staiger, p. 134.
[2] *Der Dichter*, p. 86.
[3] Howald-Staiger, p. 384.
[4] *Der Dichter*, pp. 58 f.

When the foundations of Howald's edifice crumble, the forbearance and anger of Demeter simply cannot induce us to 'long for her and fear her at the same time'. I have no wish to pillory any scholar; I have tried, in the course of this study, to record opposing views only where I felt that there was something to be learnt from our disagreement. So it is here. I suspect that Howald is reading into H. 6 the atmosphere of H. 5 (which he does not treat in his study). In the latter Kallimachos leaves us in no doubt of the uneasy calm of the midday scene. Since he is capable of exciting reactions in us, we are entitled to look for a differing purpose in a parallel poem which does not exploit the same techniques.

The truth, I prefer to think, is that to the poet feeling is a matter of form. Let us look, for example, at lines 79-81 and 105-6 of H. 5:

τὸν δὲ χολωσαμένα περ ὅμως προσέφασεν Ἀθάνα·
'τίς σε, τὸν ὀφθαλμὼς οὐκέτ' ἀποισόμενον,
ὦ Εὐηρείδα, χαλεπὰν ὁδὸν ἄγαγε δαίμων;'

νῦν δὲ κομίζευ
ὦ Εὐηρείδα, τέλθος ὀφειλόμενον.

Taken in the context of the entire poem, these lines are intended to have a pitying tone. What makes it so? *It is not the words.* In the latter lines, 'Now receive the debt owed to you, son of Everes', the thought of the *words* strikes one as brutal. We cannot look for pity in ὀφειλόμενον, for it is neutral; at H. 4. 165-6 Apollo cannot be born at Kos, for another god, Ptolemy Philadelphos, is owed by the Fates to the island (ἐκ Μοιρέων . . . . . .ὀφειλόμενος). It is just possible that there are plaintive overtones in the combination of τέλθος ὀφειλόμενον (τέλθος being a rare form of τέλος which recurs only at H. 6. 77). In Greek epitaphs death is sometimes described as the repayment of a debt, and both ὀφείλειν and τέλος occur in this connexion. For the former we may compare Call. *Epigr.* 16. 4 [1], for the latter such examples as Kaibel, *Epigr. Graeca* 613, 6 (Rome) πνεῦμα λαβὼν δάνος οὐρανόθεν τελέσας χρόνον ἀντα-πέδωκα; *I.G.* 12, 7, 119 (Amorgos) τὸ τέλος ἀπέδωκα; *I.G.* 12, 7, 120 (Amorgos) τὸ τέλος λυκάμαντι ἀπέδωκα ('I have paid my debt to

---

[1] Cf. Simonides *Anth. Pal.* x. 105. 2; Eur. *Alc.* 782, Fr. 10; Palladas *Anth. Pal.* xi. 62. See also B. Lier, *Philol.* 62 (1903), 578-583; R. Lattimore, *Themes in Greek and Latin Epitaphs* (Univ. of Illinois Press 1942), pp. 170 f. Cahen (*Comm.*, p. 238) had already cited Kaibel no. 387: τὸ δ' ὀφειλό-μενον ἀπέδωκε τῇ φύσει τέλος.

time'); Pind. *Nem.* 7. 44. But the ideas are essentially different. Teiresias owes no debt; rather, Athene is repaying a debt which the Fates have owed.

The earlier lines confront us with the fact that to reputable scholars the thought is prompted by unadulterated anger. F. L. Lucas [1] translates: 'But, in anger, Athene's voice rose ringing:'; C. del Grande [2]: 'Sdegnata gli si rivolse Atena'; Howald-Staiger: 'Dennoch aber ergrimmte und sprach zu ihm Pallas Athene'. J. G. Frazer [3] paraphrases: 'The goddess cried out in anger . . .' According to the interpretation of these scholars, ὅμως answers οὐκ ἐθέλων in line 78, and the participle plus *per* has intensive, rather than concessive, force. In total effect this interpretation recalls Ovid *Trist.* II. 105-6:

> *inscius* Actaeon uidit sine ueste Dianam:
> praeda fuit canibus *non minus* ille suis.

Anger or pity? I do not think that Kallimachos regards it an open question. He has, to be sure, set a trap for the unwary, for the progressive unveiling of a humane Athene has not *at this stage* reached the point where the reader knows of Athene's motives. The poet is mischievously inviting us to be tricked by the thought of the words, in conjunction with our own (erroneous) assessment of the situation. If we fall into the trap, and find anger in the words, we would solemnly be informed that we looked in the wrong place. Firstly, we would be told, I imagine, that 'You should know that I prefer to use participles accompanied by περ with concessive force'. It is worth recalling the extant examples:

Fr. 55.2 Ἄργος ἔθειν, ἴδιόν περ ἐὸν λάχος.
   '(Hera unloosed the Nemean lion) to ravage Argos, *although* it was her personal estate.'

H. 1.24 πολλὰ δὲ Καρίωνος ἄνω διεροῦ περ ἐόντος
   ἰλυοὺς ἐβάλοντο κινώπετα.
   'And many a serpent above Karion, wet *though* it now is, cast its lair.'

H. 1.58 τῷ τοι καὶ γνωτοὶ προτερηγενέες περ ἐόντες
   οὐρανὸν οὐκ ἐμέγηραν ἔχειν ἐπιδαίσιον οἶκον.

---

[1] *Greek Poetry for Everyman* (1951), p. 300.
[2] *Filologia Minore* (1956), p. 251.
[3] Apollodorus, Loeb edtn., I p. 363 n. 1.

'Wherefore your kindred, *although* born earlier, did not grudge that you should have heaven for your appointed abode.'

H. 3.159 οὐ γὰρ ὅ γε Φρυγίη περ ὑπὸ δρυὶ γυῖα θεωθεὶς
παύσατ' ἀδηφαγίης·

'For *although* his body was deified beneath a Phrygian oak, (Herakles) did not cease from gluttony.'

H. 3.222 οὐδὲ μὲν Ὑλαῖόν τε καὶ ἄφρονα Ῥοῖκον ἔολπα
οὐδέ περ ἐχθαίροντας ἐν Ἄιδι μωμήσασθαι
τοξότιν.

'Nor do I imagine that Hylaios and Rhoikos, *although* they hate her, slight Artemis' archery in Hades.'

H. 5.113 ὁππόταν οὐκ ἐθέλων περ ἴδῃ χαρίεντα λοετρά
δαίμονος.

'When he sees, *although* against his will, a goddess's lovely bath.'

Fr. 260.52 ναὶ τοῦτο τὸ δένδρεον αὖον ἐόν περ.

'Verily, by this staff, *for all its dryness.*'

The context, and precise meaning, of the oath are obscure, but Trypanis and Howald-Staiger see no impediment to our taking αὖον ἐόν περ as concessive.

Secondly, he would draw attention to the form.

1. Notice the sonority of line 79: $-\cup\cup\,|\,\acute{ο}\ \cup\cup\,|\,\acute{α}\ \cup\cup\,|\,\acute{ο}\ \cup\cup\,|\,\acute{α}\ \cup\cup\,|\,\acute{α}\bar{α}$. It is charged with violent emotion.

2. In line 81 we notice the spondaeic heaviness of ὦ Εὐηρείδα. A double spondee occurs at the beginning of only 9 % of hexameters and 13 % of pentameters in this poem, the least frequent combination. It is clearly used for special effect. Perhaps this is the reason why we hear now of Everes for the first time. 'A Theban nymph (57) .. mother of Teiresias (58) ... Chariklo by name (67) .. wife of Everes (81). A mythological handbook would have told us all this in one line. Perhaps here the poet is husbanding his effects as much as following a preference for the indirect; an earlier reference to Everes could have diminished the value of the useful long syllables.

3. In line 81 the metrical ictus falls in three successive syllables on the sonorous long alpha: $-\,-\,|\,-\,-\,|\,\acute{α}\ \cup\cup\,|\,\acute{α}\ \cup\cup\,|\,\acute{α}\ \cup\cup\,|\,-\,-$.

These three points express sonority and solemnity, but are not in themselves capable of differentiating pitying grief and anger. There are, however, others.

4. The thought of ὁδὸν ἄγαγε δαίμων is not necessarily pitying.
If the last two words are normally used in contexts in which an
aberration or mischance leads to calamity for the speaker or
another, Antinoos has quite different feelings towards Odysseus
at *Od.* 17.446:

τίς δαίμων τόδε πῆμα προσήγαγε, δαιτὸς ἀνίην;

But the arrangement of dentals and palatals seems to be involved in the poet's scheme. On what precise principle I do not
know, but we find the sequence d/g/g/d again at H. 6.17 δάκρυον
ἄγαγε Δηοῖ (where grief is explicit in the context), and a similar,
although not identical, usage in *Epigr.* 2.1-2 ἐς δέ με δάκρυ/ἤγαγεν
(d/d-g/g). We shall see in the next chapter that the moods of
H. 5 and H. 6.1-17 are one; if this conclusion is accepted, then
the coincidence of the pattern in 5.81 and 6.17 becomes highly
significant. There is nothing identical in more general contexts
(such as fr. 300; 384.29). We find a reversed sequence (but with
unvoiced palatals) in H. 6.41 καλὰ δένδρεα κόπτει, descriptive
of anger.

5. Above all—and this is the feature which makes 79-81 different—
at line 80 Kallimachos has ordered his material so that direct
speech opens on the gentle pentameter, rather than on the epic
hexameter. When Propertius (I. 7.19) calls the pentameter
mollis, and Hermesianax (fr. 7.35 f. Powell) calls it μαλακός,
one of the associations of the words is surely 'delicate'. It seems
to me that there is an equation between the direct speech opening
on the non-epic part of the couplet, with its more delicate effects,
and the non-epic reactions which Athene evinces. Obviously,
if this is an effect, it demands sparing use. This is the only occasion on which it occurs in direct speech in the poem; it occurs in
narrative at lines 38 (expressly pathetic) and 40 (an aftermath of
38, but inaugurating the midday disquiet). The arrangement of
thought in 80 tends to confirm this belief. In the opening trochee
the two forces are dramatically and pathetically confronted,
τίς σε. As a *unit* this surely suggests pity, not anger. We also
notice the priority of interests supplied by the thought of τὸν
ὀφθαλμὼς οὐκέτ' ἀποισόμενον; in this place *formally* it can suggest
only pitiful, or pleasurable, anticipation of his future loss.

From all this I conclude that form is the means by which Kallimachos prefers to express feeling. He might have followed Sopho-

kles, *O.T.* 1299-1302: τίς σ', ὦ τλῆμον,/προσέβη μανία; τίς ὁ πηδήσας/
μείζονα δαίμων τῶν μακίστων/πρὸς σῇ δυσδαίμονι μοίρᾳ;
There τλῆμον and δυσδαίμονι put the feelings of the speaker beyond
dispute. But it was precisely the *obviousness* of the emotional
references of tragedy from which the poet, and his confrères,
rebelled. He has devised at formal level in 79-81 what passes for
the expression of pity in his mind, and is, I suspect, so certain of
the effect being (ultimately) appreciated that at 105-6 he believes
ὦ Εὐηρείδα is sufficient to infuse into quite a callous utterance the
spirit of the former passage.

It would be useless to pretend that we react with wholehearted
satisfaction to the poet's viewpoint. There is so much shallowness
and superficiality, questions of form, not of feeling. To give another
illustration. The eleven lines devoted to Athene's love for Chariklo
at H. 5.57-67 are the poet's way of underlining the depth of the
bond which united them. But how does he deal with the situation?
He takes us on a geographical excursion. Athene and the nymph are
inseparable; hence he may take us on a tour of Boeotia with them,
and at the same time express their intimacy by not limiting the
association to Thebes, air his knowledge and avoid the oppressive
heaviness of eleven lines in monochrome. This last point seems to
me important. Even when Kallimachos is treating a pseudo-tragic
theme he divorces himself entirely from sentimentality.

The device is probably not Callimachean, but Hellenistic. This,
at any rate, is suggested by Theokritos' 13th Idyll (10-13), in a
description of Herakles' love for Hylas:

> 'And Herakles was never parted from him; neither when the Day rose
> to its zenith, nor when the white steeds of Dawn galloped up to Zeus'
> house, nor when the chirping chickens scurried to their bed on the smoky
> hen-roost at the flapping of their mother's wings.'

To some—for example, Gercke and Cholmeley—the similarity of
χωρὶς δ' οὐδέποκ' ἦς (*Id.* 13.10) to καὶ οὔποκα χωρὶς ἔγεντο (H. 5.59)
suggested that Kallimachos is drawing upon Theokritos. This is
hardly likely when similarity is limited to the idea of inseparability.
Theokritos concentrates on a phase of the education of Hylas.
His lines are merely an elaboration of the simple idea of 'morning,
noon and night'. In Kallimachos things are quite different. But if
there can be no question of literary dependence, at the same time
we may suspect that the technique owes something to a general
attitude to sentiment.

We must not expect too much of Kallimachos. We do not look in his Hymns for the destiny or dignity of man, for *lacrimae rerum*. His is armchair poetry. Konrat Ziegler, in an important article [1], has illustrated the gulf which separates Kallimachos from the erotic poets, a gulf which becomes more apparent through J. Carrière's examination [2] of the emotional range of Apollonios in the third book of the *Argonautica*. In Kallimachos we meet, in Ziegler's phrase, 'ein Nicht-ernst-nehmen-können (oder auch Nicht-ernst-nehmen-wollen)'. Unfortunately, he is prepared to pass beyond the simple stage of reticence and with a distasteful sourness ride roughshod over our finer feelings. This may be illustrated by his treatment of the bond between parent and child.

In H. 6 the feelings of Triopas and his wife towards Erysichthon are a painful travesty. Their first recorded reaction to the affliction of their son is *shame* (αἰδόμενοι, 73). This is the feeling which really prompts the mother's endless pretexts when her son is invited out, and that the poet intends us to make this identification is evident from the close of the tale. *For Erysichthon's parents the public spectacle of a king's son begging at the crossroads is the final crushing blow.* They are presented to us as a bourgeois royal family who react more strongly to the exposure of their shame, the skeleton (almost literal) in the palace cupboard, than they do to Erysichthon's personal suffering and his final autophagy. It is not a question of Kallimachos' having no further interest in the development of the original story after 'the detailed picture of insatiable hunger' [3]; if this were the whole story, the tale could have moved to its natural close. No, Kallimachos has designed an earlier climax. The autophagy cannot make his parents feel any worse.

Kallimachos creates this effect with some care. For example, this is the only point at which we are told that Triopas is a king. It was, of course, common knowledge to anyone conversant with the story, but as far as the poet's design was concerned, this was the point at which its disclosure was most effective. It is a king's son who is reduced to common beggar; the parents' disgrace is underlined. When we grasp this the sham and heavy irony of the plaintive line 83 becomes obvious:

δειλαία φιλότεκνε, τί δ'οὐκ ἐψεύσαο, μᾶτερ;

[1] 'Kallimachos und die Frauen', *Die Antike* 13 (1937), 20-42.
[2] *Euphrosyne* 2 (1959), 41-63.
[3] L. Deubner, *N.Jbb.* 1921, pp. 374-5.

The mother who is *aidomene* at 73, is—with feeling for the comic element in incongruity—described as *philoteknos* at 83. This leaves an unpleasant taste in my mouth. I once hoped that the poet was resorting to parody, for with a change of verb the line could fit a pathetic treatment of Demeter's search for Kore. But lines of an identical pattern recur at H. 4.197 and 215. No, the thought is Kallimachos', and serio-comic to the point of iconoclasm; the humour bears the brand of *epichairekakia*.

Is the irony also present in H. 5? Certainly not on the surface, for the poet had too much to lose. But I wonder whether line 90 contains more than meets the eye. When Chariclo shrieks that she will never cross Helikon again, I ask 'Why?' In genuine tragedy we would never think to ask the question; the mountain as the painful scene of the blinding of her son explains itself. But I wonder whether even here Kallimachos is guarding himself against rebuke for maudlin sentiment by directing the captious Hellenistic critic to another explanation. The stories of Teiresias and Aktaion, as has been observed, have been carefully tailored to a single pattern. Now Aktaion's mother must wander over the mountain collecting his scattered bones from every thicket. Surely Kallimachos is being perverse: since Helikon keeps Teiresias' eyes, his mother will run the gruesome risk of stepping on them. I wish that it were not required to introduce this new and depressing dimension into Hs. 5 and 6, but I think it justified. At the same time it should be stated that it is a feature of his burlesque, rather than of the Teiresias tale. We may read the latter without ever asking the question, but I think that the poet has provided for all contingencies.

These remarks on Kallimachos' preoccupation with form are intended merely to redress a loss of balance in the interpretation of the Hymns. The poet's mischief is a delightful enough experience to warrant continued study of Kallimachos. But there is more that can be said for him. If I cannot accept Howald's thesis, I nevertheless do not feel automatically driven into the arms of W. W. Tarn, who has committed himself to the depressing opinion that 'in all his (Kallimachos') fastidious variations on a dead mythology—dead even in his day to the educated [Surely an exaggeration]—there is scarcely a line with a human touch, and certainly not a line which ever made anyone's pulse beat. He is form without substance' [1]. For while there is a concern for form which gives the

---

[1] *Hellenistic Civilization* (3rd. edtn., London 1952), p. 275.

lie to the sincerity of the emotion generated by the poet, I concede him moments of high success in capturing the moods of devotion. Can the scholarly pulse really be so sluggish that it does not quicken to the excitement of the opening of Hs. 2 and 5, to the tension, yes, passion (when the word is properly applied to the poetry, and not the poet), in the first lines of H. 6?

Personally I find Kallimachos most persuasive in another direction which has hardly excited comment—his ability to create a picture of the simple faith that moves mountains. If I am right in my chronology, he tries this first in H. 2.9-11:

> 'Not to all does Apollo appear, but only to the good. Whoever sees him, he is great; who sees him not is of low estate. We shall see you, Farworker, and we shall never be lowly.'

This is not his more successful venture [1], for the atmosphere is not sharply enough defined to remove suspicions that the thoughts are thoroughly smug. It is hard to divorce the cult scene from Kallimachos' joy at the expulsion of his rival by the earthly Apollo. But H. 6.120 ff. is a nobler composition:

> 'As horses four and fair of mane the holy Basket bring,
> So shall the goddess of mighty sway come offering us fair spring,
> 　　Fair summer, winter, autumn too,
> 　　And guard us till the year is new.
> And as we trudge the city streets, our feet and heads unbared,
> So shall we always keep our feet and heads from suffering spared'

I venture a verse translation, for the passage needs the adjunct of rhythm to make us fully conscious of its liturgical qualities. It is a minor catechism; the narrator rehearses the articles of her belief. It is a simple faith. We notice the direct and naive relationship between things done, even things seen, and the goddess's grace. This spirit is abundantly suited to the role of sight and deed in the last stages of the Thesmophoria, when the goddess made her revelations in her temple. It is a robust faith. 'She shall come . . . she shall guard . . we shall have . . .' Unless I am very much mistaken, we momentarily forget the finesse of lines 120-122, the opposition of four horses to four seasons, of fair horses to fair

---

[1] I do not take Kuiper seriously when he comments (*Studia Callimachea*, I p. 194): 'Quantum languescunt versus 9-11 . . . . , quam repit humi sermo exilis et iteratione tardus!' His following words show that he is really only piqued that the poet has frustrated his search for a wealth of 'dictio epica' at this point.

seasons, the underlying image of Demeter ὡρηφόρος, 'bringer of the seasons', which the poet has borrowed from the Homeric Hymn to Demeter. We see only the primitive—so very primitive and yet so modern—sacramentalism of the cult. Literary artistry is swallowed up in naive naturalness. As I have suggested in Chapter II, at line 127 the effect is sabotaged by a verbal play, deliberately recalling the reader to the poet's wish not to be taken too seriously:

'And as the bearers of the vans bear vans with gold replete,
So may we gold unstinted- eat.'

A FLIGHT OF FANCY: THE LYDE OF ANTIMACHOS

I close this chapter with some highly speculative theorizing. It has nothing to do with my main arguments, and I hope that the reader will treat it as an aside. The thoughts have sprung from my study of H. 5.79-81 and 105-6, hence I add them to this chapter.

There is something intriguing about lines which depend upon knowledge of a poet's style, and a close attention to the form, for a definition of their mood. The situation must surely be unique. I find myself wondering whether there was an ulterior motive, beyond mere mischief, at the back of their use. What adds fuel to my fire is the fact that we know this version of the Teiresias story associated only with Pherekydes, but to the poet 'it is not my tale, but *others*". Now even if we had the full text of Pherekydes, instead of the sorry summary provided in the *Bibliotheca*, it would still be a *prose* source. How much would be added to our understanding of the lines in question, if the theme had been handled in verse, above all in elegiacs—and had, in Kallimachos' opinion, been handled badly. Had the thought of 79-81 and/or 105-6 occurred in earlier work which echoed the unexplained brutality of the Pherecydean tale, then the lines of Kallimachos could be seen as an attempt to teach the offending author his business.

There is a work which makes my last paragraph not quite the excursion into fantasia that it may seem, namely the *Lyde* of Antimachos. This poet has rightly been called 'an Alexandrian born before his time' [1]. Plutarch (*Cons. Apollon.* 9) tells us that 'when his wife Lyde died, whom he loved dearly, Antimachos wrote, as a consolation for his grief, the elegiac poem called *Lyde*, *in which he enumerated heroic sufferings, lessening his own grief*

---

[1] Edmonds, *Elegy and Iambus*, I p. 35.

by means of the ills of others.' It is clear that the occasion, whether real or imaginary, served to introduce a display of erudition, rather than genuine grief. 'Il voulait ainsi, dit Plutarque, se consoler de son chagrin. L'effort n'a pas dû être bien grand', is Couat's dry comment [1]. What interests us is that here was a precursor of the Hellenistic tradition, who wrote in elegiacs a catalogue of the sufferings of heroes and heroines.

It would seem that Antimachos' treatment of his material was quite lugubrious; at least, Hermesianax (fr. 7.45-6 Powell) tells us γόων δ' ἐνεπλήσατο βίβλους/ἱρὰς ἐκ παντὸς παυσάμενος καμάτου. The work, of which two books are known, was long enough to invite Agatharchides to write an epitome of it [2]. Antimachos' *Thebais* ran to at least 23 books, and the ancient verdict that he was prolix and garrulous [3] may apply equally to both works. Rather more important is the verdict of Quintilian (x. 1.53), that Antimachos was deficient in pathos (*adfectibus*), sweetness, arrangement of matter and art in general, for these are precisely the canons which seem of special importance in the *Bath of Pallas*. We know that Kallimachos did not think much of the *Lyde*: Λύδη καὶ παχὺ γράμμα καὶ οὐ τορόν (fr. 398), 'bloated and obscure'.

Now if Kallimachos ever had occasion to parody Antimachos, it would not be pure antiquarianism, for Antimachos' poetry and its merits were live issues in the Hellenistic period. Pfeiffer ad Call. fr. 398 points out that Kallimachos' contemporaries, Asklepiades (*Anth. Pal.* ix. 63) and Poseidippos (*Anth. Pal.* xii. 168) both commend the *Lyde*, and that both are in the company of the *Telchines*, the critics whom Kallimachos attacked so devastatingly in the preface to his *Aitia* [4]. E. A. Barber [5] even entertains the idea that the celebrated literary dispute in which Kallimachos was involved may have arisen, early in his career, over the merits of Antimachos' poetry. It would not surprise me if Antimachos had treated the story of Teiresias (in the Pherecydean version because it suited his purpose better), and had displayed his usual

---

[1] *La Poésie Alexandrine*, p. 66.
[2] Phot. *Bibl.* 171 a 24.
[3] Plut. *Garr.* 21 (*Mor.* 513 B). Cf. B. Wyss, *Antimachi Colophonii Reliquiae* (Berlin 1936), p. xix: 'Laudatur liber secundus (sc. Lydes) a Stephano Byzantio (Ant. fr. 72), sed illud παχὺ γράμμα plurium fuisse librorum veri similius est'.
[4] V. Schol. Flor. 4 f. ad fr. 1.
[5] *Oxford Classical Dictionary*, p. 157.

lack of feeling and turgidity; Kallimachos set about improving upon his presentation of material as a sort of 'class exercise' in criticism. I realize that a proliferation of possibilities falls far short of certainty, but there is another feature of the *Lyde* which should not be overlooked—the avowed intention of the work was to enable Antimachos to remember that *he could have been worse off*. This is a theme which has a special place in the *Bath of Pallas*, in the opposition of the stories of Teiresias and Aktaion.

I have been trying to show that additional knowledge could radically change our attitude to particular lines of the poem. Let me add a reference to line 82: ἁ μὲν ἔφα, παιδὸς δ'ὄμματα νὺξ ἔλαβεν. This is a seemingly inoffensive line whose delicacy has been widely appreciated. *And yet only two letters have to be changed to produce the cruelty of the Pherecydean version*:

ἁ μὲν ἔφα, παιδὸς δ' ὄμματ' ὀνυξὶ λάβεν

When I first noticed this, I was human enough to want to rush the emendation into the text of Hymn 5, in defiance of the subdued tone of line 78, for I imagined that the defiance might be the poet's, rather than my own. But I am now convinced that it is unwise to multiply blemishes in a work of such studied effect. And yet the devastating effect wrought by the change of two letters is still at least curious. Now had Antimachos used the line in its savage form, the minor change on Kallimachos' part would show the way in which a real Hellenist thought that the idea should be treated.

'So she spoke. .' in fact leads more easily into a verb of action, and is represented in the parallel structure of H. 6 by line 65: ἁ μὲν τόσσ' εἰποῖσ' 'Ερυσίχθονι τεῦχε πονηρά. 6.65 (like the 5.82 of 'Antimachos') is 5.82 of Kallimachos *in a context from which pity is absent*. Perhaps Ovid understood his Kallimachos better than some moderns, when he handled the thought of 6.65 ff.:

> moliturque genus poenae *miserabile, si non*
> *ille suis esset nulli miserabilis actis,*
> pestifera lacerare Fame [1].

Moreover, if the development that I have suggested actually did take place, there would be even more to admire in Kallimachos' adjustment, for νὺξ ἔλαβεν would preserve a nuance of the original

---

[1] *Met.* 8. 782-4.

verb of action: 'night seized' instead of 'Athene seized', and at the same time represent a particular idiom, with which we may compare Aesch. *Pers.* 365: εὖτ' ἂν . . . κνέφας . . . τέμενος αἰθέρος λάβῃ, i.e. 'night occupied his eyes'.

If I am right, this will explain Kallimachos' initial interest in the Pherecydean version, and enrich our understanding of particular lines; whether many or none, only the shifting sands of Egypt can reveal [1].

---

[1] For example, we would like to know whether Ant. fr. 72 (φεύγοντας γαίης ἔκτοθι Δωτιάδος) really does refer to the Thessalian migration to Knidos, as Stoll conjectured. Wyss ad loc. (p. 39) comments: 'Fieri potest, ut A. perinde atque Callimachus hanc rem in describendis Cereris erroribus perstrinxerit; cf. fr. 67'. If Ant. fr. 72 is on the same theme as Call. H. 6.24, the possibilities become doubly exciting.

PROLEGOMENA TO CHAPTER SIX

On pp. 111 ff. I make a suggestion about Kallimachos' possible use of Philitas' *Demeter*, of course incapable of proof. There is, however, one significant pointer, which I have belatedly observed through some remarks of K. Keyssner, *Gottesvorstellung und Lebens-auffassung im Griechischen Hymnus* (1932), p. 61. When discussing a feature of hymnal style, that 'the thought that a god has received his τιμή from another is often formulated with the help of πάρ and ἐκ', he introduces Philitas fr. 2 (Powell, *Coll. Alex.* p. 90): ἀλλ' ὅτ' ἐπὶ χρόνος ἔλθῃ, ὃς ἐκ Διὸς ἄλγεα πέσσειν / ἔλλαχε, καὶ πενθέων φάρμακα μοῦνος ἔχει.

'Die Zeit erhielt von Zeus die Macht, die Schmerzen zu lindern'. (For ἔλλαχε in association with divinities, see Keyssner, p. 64 f.)

The time which is accorded this quasi-deification can only be that of Demeter's ending of her mourning, precisely the time for which Kallimachos has introduced a new mythological role for Hesperos (see p. 108 *infra*). Surely this can not be pure coincidence.

CHAPTER SIX

HYMN 6: THE GROUNDPLAN

Hs. 5 and 6 have a common structure. This fact is generally acknowledged, but I have yet to find a thorough analysis of what the statement means. We shall see that the question not only reinforces the interpretation that I have placed upon H. 5, but also leads to conclusions for H. 6.

The sixth hymn, addressed to Demeter, also involves a procession, a group of devotees, a cautionary tale and what may very roughly be called an epiphany. It is presumably the close of the second phase of the *Thesmophoria*, a festival in honour of Demeter which was celebrated throughout the Greek world. The Sacred Basket (*Kalathos*) is expected in procession, to mark the end of the women's mourning and fasting, and the beginning of an exultant mood which the revelations on the final day of the mystery cult festival inspired. The atmosphere is intense, for the women have been fasting all day, it is mystery religion and the hour of their release is at hand. As they wait the narrator tells the tale of Erysichthon 'so that one may avoid transgression' (ἵνα καί τις ὑπερβασίας ἀλέηται, 22).

Where is the festival being celebrated? Kallimachos does not tell us. And yet for the locale of the Bath of Pallas he speaks clearly and, in the Hellenistic manner, diffusely. We are left in no doubt that it is Argos. Argos is mentioned (45, 140), also the Argives (36). Those who remember from their mythology that Arestor was the father of Argos, the eponym of the city, are reminded of the noble clan of the Arestoridai (34); also of the place of Danaos in Argive tradition (48, 142). Pelasgiades (4), Pelasgos (51) and Achaiiades (13) are epic equivalents for 'Argive'. Diomedes (35) is the national hero of Argos, and Inachos its principal river (50, 140). For those with a knowledge of local geography, which we do not now share, there were Mt. Kreion and the springs Physadeia and Amymone (40, 41; 47-8). (The latter are also numbered among the four Argive (*Pelasgiades*) springs at fr. 66.7-9.) The reason for the poet's insistence we have already seen; it is the Argive cult of

Athene Oxyderkes which is intended to give meaning to the focal point, the 'cautionary' tale.

The knowledge that Kallimachos was using the locale of H. 5 in a special way suggests that, when the poet carefully avoids giving precise reference to place in H. 6, it is because we are not encouraged to waste time in looking for a similar idea in it. The Thesmophoria was a festival widespread throughout the Greek world [1], probably also a Kalathos procession [2]. They suggested no one locale rather than another. Undoubtedly the poet had opportunity to observe them in Alexandria, where, according to the scholiast, Ptolemy Philadelphos had established them on the model of an Eleusinian Kalathos procession (of which we know nothing, and are suspicious). But the poet nowhere mentions Alexandria as the scene of H. 6, nor Cyrene, nor Knidos. And yet these three places have been advanced as the locale. The idea that the hymn was to be closely connected with the worship of Demeter at Knidos (where Triopas was worshipped as a hero) is thought of now as a special belief of Couat, who wrote in an age which believed that the hymns were declaimed, by invitation, in particular places. I doubt whether Knidos has a convinced modern advocate, but Prof. P. von der Mühll [3] is respectful at least to the extent of not finding the arguments against it thoroughly convincing.

The theory that Cyrene, Kallimachos' birthplace, was intended has received frequent support, most recently from F. Chamoux [4]. The idea is not surprising, for the poet obviously had close connexions with Cyrene, and archaeological discoveries and features of the local dialect helped to make the thought attractive. It is rather

---

[1] See W. Sontheimer, *R.E.* Hlbd. xi A (1936), 24 ff.

[2] A. B. Cook, *Zeus*, III. ii pp. 990 ff.; F. Sokolowski, *Lois Sacrées de l'Asie Mineure* (Paris 1955), pp. 22, 153 f.

[3] *Festschrift Ernst Kapp*, 1958, p. 109 n. 1.

[4] *Cyrène sous la monarchie des Battiades* (1953), pp. 266 f. Cf. C Anti, Africa Italiana 2 (1929), 222 ff.; L. Vitali, *Fonti per la Storia della Religione Cyrenaica* (1932), 136; Coppola, *Cirene e il nuovo Callimaco* (1935), p. 6. In his most recent publications Prof. Chamoux not only connects the hymn with Cyrene but even assigns it (and a number of other poems) to an early period before Kallimachos left the city for Alexandria: *Rev. hist.* 216 (1956), 32; *B.C.H.* 82 (1958), 587; *R.E. G.* 73.2 (1960), xxxiii f. At the lastmentioned place three reasons are summarized: the use of Doric, topographical detail and the absence of allusion to the Lagids. I have given another explanation of the first, the second is not striking in view of the vagueness of the poem while the third will carry conviction only for those who cannot conceive that the poet may have a plan of his own.

astonishing, at the same time, to find its most recent advocate
declaring that 'Kallimachos' poem is sung at the departure of the
procession' (p. 267 n. 1), without attention to the cogent—and
by now, one would have thought, historic—proofs of Ph.-E.
Legrand [1], that Hymns 2, 5 and 6 cannot be made to conform in
any way to the timing of an actual procession.

It is sometimes believed that lines 7 ff. assist us to define the
locale:

> 'Hesperos from Heaven marks the time of the coming of the Basket [2],
> Hesperos, who alone persuaded Demeter to drink when she was pursuing
> the unknown tracks of her ravished daughter. Lady, how could your feet
> bear you right to the West, right to the black men and where the golden
> apples are?'

This is held to point us to Cyrene [3], or at least to an African tradition
that 'Déméter, errant par le monde, est venue aussi par chez nous' [4].
It is more than doubtful whether it does anything of the sort.
The passage rather illustrates the deep community of feeling which
the fasting devotees share with Demeter, whose *planê* they relive.
The Evening Star has seen the Kalathos start upon its journey; he
has broader horizons than they. Since the *Nesteia* concluded with
the appearance of Hesperos, Hesperos is described as persuading
Demeter to break her fast. That is to say, a natural feature which is
given dramatic force elsewhere in Greek literature (for example,
Sappho has Hesperos call the cattle home, Kallimachos has it free
the oxen from their yokes [5]) is now given mythological status.
Hesperos, like Iambe in the canonical story, persuaded Demeter
to drink. Therefore they must have met, and, naturally enough, in
the west.

When then Kallimachos says 'West', he means no more than he
says. The rare form δυθμή (ἠελίου) for 'the west' recurs only at
Call. fr. 177.5-6, where again it is associated with Hesperos. Malten [6]
assumed a more symmetrical pattern in our poet. He placed the

---

[1]　*R.E.A.* 3 (1901), 281-312.
[2]　For the interpretation see Mair's translation, and von der Mühll, *Fest-schrift Ernst Kapp*, 1958, 109-112.
[3]　Vollgraff, *Mnem.* 42 (1914), 417 f.
[4]　Cahen, *Comm.* p. 249.
[5]　Fr. 177. 5-6. Cf. Cat. lxii. 20-21 (Hesperus wrenches the bride from her mother's embrace), on which see J. Ferguson, *Greece and Rome* (S. 2) 3 (1956), 53.
[6]　*Herm.* 45 (1910), 544.

Hesperides near Cyrene, '*im Süden*', the Ethiopians (for so the scholiast explains 'the black men') in the east, and Hesperos in the west. He writes therefore of 'einen über Süd gezogenen West-Ostbogen'. None will dispute that the Garden of the Hesperides was often placed near Cyrene [1], but here it stands for 'the west', as simply as Hesperos does. For the Ethiopians, we learn something from Verg. *Aen.* 4.480 f., where, *at the bounds of Ocean*, where *Atlas* performs his labour, is the *ultimus Aethiopum locus*, and *Hesperidum templi custos*. From Homer onwards the Ethiopians live in two isolated communities, some in the east, some in the west [2]. When Vollgraff [3] asserts that Kallimachos 'non dicit Aethiopes orientales neque vero occidentales, sed illos, qui Cyrenaicae proximi sunt', his argument is indefensible.

All three terms of reference simply stand for 'the west'. And the rest then follows naturally: 'How did your feet have the strength to take you on such a long journey, to the West? You were hungry and thirsty the while . . . Three times in fact you circled the globe, hungry and thirsty the while . .' The devotees, as is to be expected, identify themselves with the goddess in her privation and painful ordeal. It is hard not to remember, at the two poles of Christendom, the spirit of the Stations of the Cross and

'Were you there when they crucified my Lord?
                       (Were you there?)
Were you there when they crucified my Lord?
O sometimes it causes me to tremble, tremble, tremble.
Were you there when they crucified my Lord?'

At the beginning of H. 6 we seem to be breathing the same atmosphere as in H. 5. The same intense expectation, even more intense, to suit the mood of a mystery cult. And, it might seem, a more appropriate occasion—the *Nesteia*, Day of Fasting, and the moment on that day when emotions were rawest as the ritual fast drew to its close. Further, a more appropriate divinity, for Demeter, the *mater dolorosa* of the ancient world, renewed her lamentation periodically in the frequent lays of the Rape of Persephone, and annually her experience was relived in her mystery cult.

---

[1] Chamoux, *Cyrène sous la monarchie des Battiades*, pp. 226, 280.
[2] *Od.* 1. 24; Ap. Rhod. *Arg.* 3. 1192. Cf. A. Lesky, *Herm.* 87 (1959), 27-38.
[3] *Mnem.* 42 (1914), 418-9.

She is then a more enduring subject for threnody than Athene, and
we imagine that we understand why the narrator tells and retells
of her abstinence from the bath and food and drink, *and also why
Kallimachos has persisted in the use of Doric.* Threnodic elegy is to
be replaced by an epic threnody. Doric hexametric threnody would
invite us to compare Erinna's *Lament for Baukis*, the 'Lament for
Daphnis' in Theokritos' First Idyl and the anonymous *Lament for
Bion.* [1]

It was also possible that the abandonment of elegiacs might
have seemed more significant than the preservation of the dialect,
and Hs. 5 and 6 might have been contrasted in much the same way
as G. B. A. Fletcher [2] approached a problem in Ovid:

> 'Ovid's skill in narrative is apparent in his two tellings of the tale of
> Cephalus and Procris in the *Ars Amatoria* and the *Metamorphoses*. In
> the former Cephalus is *miser*, in the latter *sceleratus*. The former story, in
> which Procris's unthinking passion is the ultimate cause of her death, is
> suited to elegiac verse, the latter, in which fault is put upon Cephalus,
> is suited to epic.'

Kallimachos deliberately recalls us to the tone of H. 5 in his use of
effects. There is crisp palatal alliteration in lines 1, 3, 5, 9, 15, 17.
Long alpha and omega are used to advantage in lines 6: αὐαλέων
στομάτων πτύωμες (-∪∪ | ό ∪∪ | ό - | ό ∪) and 14: ἀενάων ποταμῶν
ἐπέρασας (ά ∪∪ | ό ∪∪ | ό ∪∪ | ά ∪). Line 10, with its alliterative
filigree of interlaced palatals and dentals, breathes a tenderness
which is more at home in elegy:

πότνια, πῶς σε δύναντο πόδες φέρεν ἔστ' ἐπὶ δυθμάς.

But, mischievously, he has been imposing upon our analysis
of the fifth hymn; he has set us off to a false start. 'Let us not,
not tell of those things which brought tears to Demeter'. We are
instead to sing of the Joys of Demeter, how she brought grain and
its cultivation to mankind, how she trained Triptolemos to transmit
her gift. For the mood is now one of joy and triumph. The devotees
and other women of good will who have fasted in her honour are to
receive their reward, the uninitiated in the experience of the kalathos
procession, the initiates in her revelations in her temple. At sunset,
the mood has changed, and the poet has cut his cloth accordingly.

---

[1] Cf. Bowra, *Greek Poetry and Life* (Gilbert Murray Festschrift 1936),
337 = *Problems in Greek Poetry* 1953, 163.
[2] *Proc. Class. Assoc.* 54 (1957), 24.

Now and again—as with the *Lyde* of Antimachos in Ch. V—it is
necessary to take bold steps in the dark, in the hope that those
who follow will enjoy a better plotted course, or at least avoid a
pitfall which has engulfed the guide. My next page or two is explora-
tory speculation of this kind, and is not essential to the argument.
It concerns the function of lines 13-15.

The idea that Kallimachos' short summary of the Rape of Persephone draws upon a fuller treatment in his *Aitia*—the view of
Malten and others—is neither convincing nor fruitful. It could
with the greatest profit derive from Philitas' *Demeter*. The summary
contains two individualistic features. Firstly, Demeter laments at
the well *Kallichoron* (15), whereas in the Homeric Hymn the well
Parthenion, by which she sits (99), and the Kallichoron, by which
her rites are established (270 ff.), are kept distinct. Secondly,
Demeter travels three times round the world. There is nothing like
this in the Homeric Hymn, in which the goddess spends nine days
(47 ff.) in her travels before being enlightened by Helios, and an
indeterminate period thereafter before reaching Eleusis. Since it is
the nine day period which is first connected with Demeter's fasting
and abstention from the bath (49-50; cf. Call. H. 6. 12, 16), 'three
times round the world' is likely to be a refinement upon 'nine days
on her travels'. Each of these two points has been explained separa-
tely; we shall look at them individually first, to get our bearings on
contemporary discussion, and then see what conclusions may
follow if we think of *both* of them as signposts in a special direction.

The territory of the wells of Eleusis was thoroughly traversed
in 1942 by G. E. Mylonas [1]. His conclusions were novel, and attractive. A well in the N.E. corner of the Greater Propylaea at Eleusis is
the Parthenion of the Homeric Hymn. A well by the N. E. corner
of the stoa of Philo was originally Kallichoron, but after it became
filled in, perhaps at the close of the Archaic period, the name was
transferred to the Parthenion. The correct name of the latter then
disappeared. Mylonas discusses in evidence Eur. *Suppl.* 391-2, and
Paus. 1, 38, 6, and for the idea that Demeter mourned by *Kallichoron*, our passage in Kallimachos, [Apollodoros] (1.5.1) and
Nikandros (*Ther.* 484-7).

On the function of the triple circuit of the world, there have been

---

[1] *The Hymn to Demeter and Her Sanctuary at Eleusis* (St. Louis 1942),
pp. 64-81.

a number of verdicts. Malten [1] saw it as an exaggeration which impressively underlines Demeter's agony in her long and unsuccessful wandering. Wilamowitz [2] thought of it as an amusing pious exaggeration, which rightly offended Kleinknecht [3], who saw it as another example of the practice of magnifying the physique, achievements, etc. of divinity (*barock-grossartig*). Herter [4] regarded it as 'eine barockale Steigerung, die in den emotionellen Äusserungen der durstenden Frauen eine starke Wirkung tut'. Lastly, Howald [5] finds an illustration, not only of pious exaggeration, but also of 'how primitive is the knowledge of the female narrator, especially in regard to geography'. All are agreed on one thing, that the poet has exaggerated.

Mylonas' conclusions on Parthenion and Kallichoron are convincing, but there is one point of special interest, the fact that we have to go to Kallimachos (twice—here and at fr. 611: Καλλιχόρῳ ἐπὶ φρητὶ καθέζεο παιδὸς ἄπυστος), Nikandros and [Apollodoros] to find Demeter sitting by Kallichoron, in defiance of the tradition of the Homeric Hymn, which our poet clearly uses at the beginning of H. 6. I would suspect that there is an intermediary Hellenistic source, a scholar who may well have known of the change of nomenclature, but above all found Kallichoron more euphonous. Kallimachos builds upon it for palatal alliteration (Καλλιχόρῳ χαμάδις ἐκαθίσσαο), just as the author of the Homeric Hymn had done before him (272 Καλλιχόρου καθύπερθεν ἐπὶ προὔχοντι κολωνῷ. Cf. also Ap. Rh. 2.904.)

Philitas' poem enjoyed great prestige among the Hellenists. Its loss is therefore the more to be regretted. We suspect—but it is no more than a suspicion—that Philitas, as a Hellenist, utilized the opportunity of discussing Demeter's travels to expatiate on out-of-the-way facts and places. If this were true, he might have found good reason to credit Demeter with more than one circuit of the globe. Wilamowitz once wrote that he had nothing to learn from scholars who talked about Antimachos and Philitas as if we knew everything about their works. Of course this is prudent; but when there are interpretations under discussion among scholars it is equally a mark of prudence to weigh every interpretation which

[1] *Herm.* 45 (1910), 544.
[2] *Hell. Dicht.* II p. 26.
[3] P. 321.
[4] *Der Dichter*, p. 56.

offers reward. For if it should prove that Philitas had utilized both Demeter's rest by Kallichoron and the triple circuit of the globe, the reference to his work by Kallimachos would serve a particular purpose.

It is this. In H. 5 we noticed the poet's use of delayed effect; it is not until the tenor of the plaintive tale becomes clear that we discover why Kallimachos has used the elegiac couplet. It would be almost impossible to anticipate the reason for its use from the beginning of the tale. I suggest that it is not until line 17 of H. 6 that we discover why he has *stopped* using the elegiac couplet. Phili-

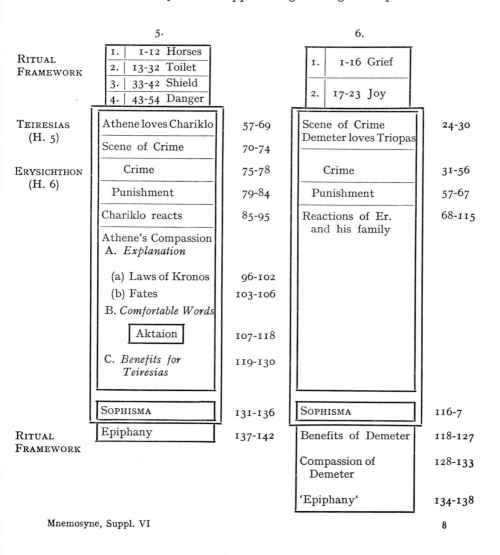

	5.		6.	
RITUAL FRAMEWORK	1. | 1-12 Horses 2. | 13-32 Toilet 3. | 33-42 Shield 4. | 43-54 Danger		1. | 1-16 Grief 2. | 17-23 Joy	
TEIRESIAS (H. 5)	Athene loves Chariklo	57-69	Scene of Crime Demeter loves Triopas	24-30
	Scene of Crime	70-74		
ERYSICHTHON (H. 6)	Crime	75-78	Crime	31-56
	Punishment	79-84	Punishment	57-67
	Chariklo reacts	85-95	Reactions of Er. and his family	68-115
	Athene's Compassion A. *Explanation* (a) Laws of Kronos	96-102		
	(b) Fates	103-106		
	B. *Comfortable Words* Aktaion	107-118		
	C. *Benefits for Teiresias*	119-130		
	SOPHISMA	131-136	SOPHISMA	116-7
RITUAL FRAMEWORK	Epiphany	137-142	Benefits of Demeter	118-127
			Compassion of Demeter	128-133
			'Epiphany'	134-138

tas wrote his *Demeter* in elegiacs. When Kallimachos turns his back
on threnody, if the Rape of Persephone were inspired by Philitas'
treatment, it would equally suggest that he turns his back on elegy
along with threnody.

Let us retreat now to safer ground, the comparative structure
of Hs. 5 and 6, which I present first in tabular form.

It is noteworthy that, while the cautionary tale of H. 6 ends at
line 117, the conclusion does not follow as swiftly as it does in H. 5
and, for that matter, the normal Homeric hymn. H. 5 has only
six lines of *envoi* (137-142), and that includes mention of the
epiphany as well as the usual prayers for future prosperity; no
Homeric hymn devotes more than six lines to its close. But H. 6
introduces an interlude of 16 lines (118-133) for the 'epiphany',
before a concluding *envoi* of five lines (134-8). Why has the poet
done this? There is the more reason to ask this question now, for a
papyrus text of the hymn (*P. Oxy.* 2226) jumps from line 117 to
138, and then starts a new verse. At this point the text is torn, but
Pfeiffer [1] entertains the possibility that a fragment of five lines
which is by the same hand should be appended here.

This omission suggests to me that there were some who felt that
after the conclusion of the cautionary tale the hymn grew top-heavy.
If this is the proper explanation, I do not think that they were
right. For when we look at the table of the elements of Hs. 5 and 6,
it becomes clear that two elements of H. 5 are missing from the
corresponding section of H. 6—the goddess's compassion and favours.
They are of course missing from the Erysichthon story, because
the villain (and the villain's family) does not qualify for them.
Instead, the poet includes them in the epiphany section:

Benefits: 'As the Basket is drawn by horses four and fair, so shall
the mighty goddess of broad domain come bringing us a fair
spring, fair summer and winter, and autumn too; she shall
guard us till the coming year. As we tread the city, bare of
head and foot, so shall we always have feet and heads unharmed.
As the bearers of the vans bear vans filled with gold, so shall
we eat (*alii*, get) gold in abundance.'

Compassion: 'The uninitiated shall follow as far as the townhall,
but the initiated right up to the goddess, those who are under
sixty years of age; but those who are burdened—both those

---

[1] Vol. II p. liii.

who stretch out hands to the Goddess of Childbirth and those who are ill—shall follow as far as they can, as far as their legs retain their vigour. Demeter will give them all her gifts in full measure as well as to those who reach the shrine.' [1]

These elements are inserted here, not simply to provide an artificial balance between H. 5 and H. 6, but because, in the case of the worship of Demeter, they are especially appropriate here. *The goddess of mystery cult shows her favours to her initiates.*

Let us return to the cautionary tale itself. The first thing that we notice is that the proper atmosphere for pity is lacking. Erysichthon is everything that Teiresias is not [2]. He is the son of Triopas, Demeter's favourite at her Thessalian grove on the Dotion plain, but, in a fit of near madness, cuts timber in the goddess's temenos to roof his banqueting hall. Demeter, in the guise of her aged priestess Nikippe, seeks to mollify him, but is roundly abused and threatened. Nemesis records his violent threat: 'Shove off, or I'll stick my great axe in your skin', and Demeter must punish him. An insatiable hunger takes possession of the offender, and despite the sufferings of his family nothing is of avail. At the end of the tale Kallimachos leaves the king's son a beggar at the crossroads, shunning for dramatic purposes the gruesome demise which we find preserved in Ovid's version (*Met.* 8.877-8), but—as I shall try to show in my later study-fully aware of it.

I have already mentioned the difference that it makes that Demeter's love is shared, and that her love for Triopas is 'dismissed' in half a line. Triopas is not her *especial* favourite; we are not invited to think of him in the way in which we have thought of Chariklo. The poem is full of parallels of this sort, underlining the essentially different situation. Erysichthon is an only son, but he is not an only child. We hear of two sisters, whose names, unfortunately, we do not know; their presence takes the edge off the sharpness of the image of the only son, for his parents will not

---

[1]   The text here is corrupt (127-8): ταῖσι δὲ Δηώ | δωσεῖ πάντ' ἐπίμεστα καὶ ὡς ποτὶ ναὸν ἵκωνται. There is no reason why we should not trust the scholiast for the meaning: ταῖς ἐλθούσαις καὶ ταῖς μὴ ἐλθούσαις ἴσον μισθὸν δώσει ἡ Δημή-τηρ. This has suggested as Kallimachos' reading, not ὡς, but αἷς = ταύταις αἵ. Barber (*C.R.* 1954, p. 229) offers ταῖς δ' (or ταῖς) ἴσα Δηώ . . . . καὶ αἷς . . . . .

[2]   If, as Kleinknecht noted, θεοφιλία is an element of H. 5 θεομαχία is its counterpart here. For θεομαχία as a technical term see W. Nestle, *Gr. Studien* (Stuttgart 1948), pp. 567-596; J. C. Kamerbeek, *Mnem.* S. IV. 1 (1948), 271-283.

be alone. His mother's name no authority has told us. Kallimachos does not oblige us, for she cannot play the part of Chariklo, and is therefore very much in the background as far as her identity is concerned. Erysichthon's offence is only indirectly connected with the satisfaction of natural needs. His offence is active (he fells), whereas Teiresias' is passive (he sees); above all, it is deliberate.

This is why Kallimachos goes out of his way to create atmosphere in H. 5.72 ff., the uneasy midday calm, whereas at H. 6.38 he is deliberately casual: τῷ ἔπι ταὶ νύμφαι ποτὶ τὥνδιον ἐψιόωντο. He will not even allow us to recreate the atmosphere of the Fifth Hymn, for he does not tell us unequivocally that this was in fact the time of day at which the outrage took place.

Demeter is as humane as Athene: 'Child, who are cutting down trees consecrated to the gods, child, cease, child, subject of your parents' many prayers, stop and turn away your servants, lest lady Demeter be angry, whose holy place you are ravaging.' (46-9). 'Child . . . child . . . child'. The aged have a tendency to talk down to the young. It is natural, but it is bad psychology, sure to create a hostile reaction. I think that Kallimachos knows this, for, after all, Demeter must not be too persuasive! The form of the punishment bears no relationship to Demeter's nature, but to the motive for the offence: 'Verily verily, build your house, you shameless dog, in which you will hold your banquets; for hereafter your carousels shall come thick and fast' (63-4). This seems to me particularly important. Whereas Demeter is traditionally endowed with the power to withhold her grain, as well as to bestow it, to make it digestible [1] as well as indigestible [2], Kallimachos has refrained from attributing the form of punishment to Demeter in a way which would recall the situation in H. 5. Athene reacts to her nature, but here Demeter reacts to stimulus.

These are not the only points at which, while the stories share a common general structure, the poet's treatment, *and therefore his purpose*, differs from that of H. 5. Triopas does not appeal to Demeter, although he is a favourite of the divinity. The situation is irremediable, and an appeal to Demeter would complicate matters, principally by making the thought sententious; it would be difficult to keep the sparkle in the burlesque. And so he appeals

---

[1] Cf. Pandareos of Ephesos, to whom Demeter gave the gift of freedom from indigestion, Anton. Lib. *Met.* 11.

[2] Cf. the lot of the offender in (Lys.) *or.* 6. 1.

to Poseidon, who does not listen. I find a good example of Kalli-machos' change of attitude in the lamentation which follows the wasting away of Erysichthon: 'His mother wept, and his two sisters groaned deeply and the breast that he sucked and the many tens of handmaids' (94-5). Whereas in H. 5 the weeping of Chariklo alone was sufficient to move Athene to pity, in H. 6 Triopas tears his hair and the whole house seems awash with tears, and yet the scene is no more piteous because of it [1]. Kallimachos may exploit the situation of Erysichthon's disease at length and ruthlessly, because none of the concomitants of proper pity are present. In the words of Chares [2]: μὴ τοὺς κακοὺς οἴκτειρε πράσσοντας κακῶς.

To call the treatment in general 'cruel' (as Cahen has done) is to obscure the vital fact that to the poet Erysichthon does not qualify for tragic treatment. In this regard it is worth noting that the only play which provides evidence of any sort for Erysichthon's appea-rance on the stage is a *satyr-play*, the *Aithon* of Achaios [3].

At this point we ask ourselves why the poet has maintained the use of Doric in H. 6. The moment that he changes course at line 17, we are debarred from finding any further relationship with threnody. For long I thought it was just an elaborate sham. The dialect which is so effective for a tragic theme is seen to be without special significance when it is wedded to a subject which lacks the elements of tragedy; that is, that it is used in a negative way, merely to complete the parallelism of Hymns 5 and 6. But this idea was wrong, for there is something positive in its use. *Doric is a dialect of more than one mood, and Doric comedy is a type whose existence is undisputed.* Now if it can be shown as reasonable that in H. 6 we have the treatment of a myth in the spirit of a Doric form of literature, the existence of which is established, then it may help to settle the question of H. 5, for which I support the idea of a Doric form of literature, the existence of which has been called into question. The degree of parallelism between the two hymns would also encourage the conclusion.

---

[1] Cf. its use in folktale, e.g. Anton. Lib. 18: ἡ δὲ μήτηρ ὡς εἶδε καὶ ὁ πατὴρ καὶ οἱ θέραπες μέγιστον ἐποιήσαντο πένθος. Kallimachos may have borrowed it from popular story telling, but is putting it to special use.

[2] Fr. 2 b 18 Diehl. Aristotle (*Poetics* 1453 a) would agree.

[3] The fragments have most recently been edited by V. Steffen, *Satyro-graphorum Graecorum Fragmenta²*, (Poznan 1952), pp. 236-7.

By Doric comedy I do not mean early Doric farce [1], with its prominent indecency; rather, the later, more refined comedy that we associate with the name of Epicharmos. Anyone who has read Miss Lever's pages [2] on him, with Kallimachos' treatment of Erysichthon in mind, cannot fail to be struck by the resemblances.

In the first place, 'many of the plays are mythological burlesques, a form popular among Dorian peoples' [3]. Odysseus and Herakles are clear favourites, each being the subject of five plays [4]. That the treatment of Erysichthon in H. 6 is mythological burlesque will not, I imagine, be gainsaid by many. Now it is interesting to notice that Herakles' ravenous appetite, the stock-in-trade of Attic comedy, already makes an appearance in Epicharmos. Athenaios (X. 411 a-b) specifically quotes a passage from the *Busiris* while on the subject of Herakles' gluttony (fr. 8 Olivieri = 21 Kaibel):

> 'In the first place, if you were to see him eating, you would die. His gullet thunders inside, his jaw rattles, his molar chomps, his canine tooth grinds, he sizzles at the nostrils, and he waggles his ears.'

The culinary fragments of the *Marriage of Hebe* (later revised as the *Muses*), in which the wedding feast of Herakles and Hebe is well to the fore, suggest that there also the theme was exploited [5]. *Hungry Erysichthon, then, is a highly suitable substitute for the gluttonous Herakles.*

This coincidence in itself would be sufficient to suggest Kallimachos' intention in H. 6, but there is probably a further parallel. 'Most of the remaining plays suggest by their titles that the characters were either abstractions or types' [6]. We could wish that we knew more about these plays, but the statement seems a reasonable inference from titles such as *'Earth and Sea'*, *'Mr. and Mrs. Reason'* (*Logos kai Logina*, which has invited comparison with Aristophanes'

---

[1]   See K. Lever, *The Art of Greek Comedy* (London 1956), pp. 15-18.

[2]   Pp. 45-53.

[3]   Lever, p. 47; cf. Pickard-Cambridge, *Dithyramb, Tragedy and Comedy*, pp. 380, 383 f.

[4]   For Odysseus see E. D. Phillips, *Greece and Rome*, S. 2. 6 (1959), 58 ff.; for Herakles Lever and Pickard-Cambridge, *locc. cit.*

[5]   Frr. 12, 18, 21, 22 Olivieri = 42, 53, 57, 58 Kaibel. For the gluttony theme see A. Olivieri, *Frammenti della Commedia Greca e del Mimo nella Sicilia e nella Magna Graecia* (Naples 1946), I p. 17.

[6]   Lever, p. 48; Pickard-Cambridge, pp. 393, 396 ff. Cf. L. Radermacher, *Aristophanes' Frösche* (1921), pp. 25 ff.

argument of Just and Unjust Reason), '*Hope or Wealth*'. At
a more modest level we find personification in *Odysseus the Deserter*
(fr. 53 O. = 101 K.):

> ἁ δ' Ἀσυχία χαρίεσσα γυνά,
> καὶ Σωφροσύνας πλατίον οἰκεῖ [1].

I think that Kallimachos knew the abstraction as a characteristic
of Epicharmos' plays, and that he made the most of it. Erysichthon
in fact invited him to do so. Hellanikos (4 F 7 Jacoby) is the first
to tell us that the villain had a nickname Aithon, ὅτι ἦν ἄπληστος
βορᾶς, an association which probably goes back to the Hesiodic
Eoiai [2]. The tradition implies that Erysichthon was called Aithon
because a violent, ravening hunger was called αἴθων λιμός. The
phrase recurs, for example, in the Eion inscription [3] and at Call.
H. 6.66-7, and I have pleaded for recognition of it at Hes. *Works and
Days*, 363. It follows that in this explanation Erysichthon and
Ravening Hunger are equated. As L. Preller and C. Robert [4]
expressed it: 'Others called him *Aithon*, that is, Ravening Hunger
personified'.

Now this is not a natural use of language. *Aithon*, 'burning', does
not contain within itself the idea of 'ravening hunger', *Heisshunger*.
It is a makeshift explanation, presented, as Th. Zielinski has clearly
shown [5], by a people who knew two stories involving violent
hunger, one featuring Erysichthon, the other an Aithon. The areas
of contact led to the amalgamation of the two, by the aid of αἴθων
λιμός. But, we should note, this amalgamation has already taken
place at the earliest point at which we encounter the story. From
that time onwards Erysichthon is nicknamed Aithon because
Ravening Hunger is *aithon*.

Kallimachos exploits this feature by drawing only the thinnest
of lines between the victim and the affliction. Let us take H. 6.116-7
as an example. Here the female narrator introduces a protestation

---

[1] See K. Lever, 'Poetic Metaphor and Dramatic Allegory in Aristophanes', *Classical Weekly* 46 (1952-3), 220-223, in which this fragment is
discussed.

[2] I have written on this in *Mnem.* S. iv. 12 (1959), 198-203. Since that
date the matter has been settled by the publication of *P.I.F.A.O.* 322
by J. Schwartz (*Pseudo-Hesiodeia*, Leiden: Brill 1960, pp. 265 ff. esp.
268, 586).

[3] *Ap.* Aeschin. *Or.* III. 183.

[4] *Gr. Myth*,[4], 1894, p. 776.

[5] *Philol.* N. F. 4 (1891), 137-162.

of her own piety. It is a traditional feature, prompted by a tale of great impiety [1]. 'Demeter, may that man be no friend of mine who is hateful to you, nor may he share the same—dividing wall. .' Do we expect this last idea, ὁμότοιχος? Surely not. We expect 'the same roof', ὁμωρόφιος or the like [2], or something like the very similar protestation of the Chorus at Soph. *Antig.* 374-5:

μήτ' ἐμοὶ παρέστιος
γένοιτο μήτ' ἴσον φρονῶν, ὃς τάδ' ἔρδει.

Instead, we have the common dividing wall. The unexpected word is, as often, a pointer to a literary reference, in this case Aesch. *Ag.* 1003-4:

νόσος γὰρ <ἀεὶ>
γείτων ὁμότοιχος ἐρείδει.

The allusion has other important consequences which I pass over now, but let us notice the subject, *nosos*. Disease is a bad neighbour when only a thin partition separates it from others and it is aggressive (ἐρείδει, it thrusts against the wall) [3]. A neighbour as hungry, and as desperate, as Erysichthon is indeed to the female speaker κακογείτων. One important conclusion to be drawn from the literary allusion is that Erysichthon, who, to begin with, was smitten with disease (μεγάλᾳ δ'ἐστρεύγετο νούσῳ, 67), is now Disease Incarnate. The idea is brilliant in its simplicity: Erysichthon wastes, the disease grows in him, the disease absorbs him.

This is the reason—as I hope to demonstrate on another occasion—why Kallimachos does not feature the personification of Hunger who appears in Ovid's version; the feature is built into the treatment of Erysichthon. We may use this point to settle the interpretation of line 102: νῦν δὲ κακὰ βούβρωστις ἐν ὀφθαλμοῖσι κάθηται. Here the poet deliberately presents us with a choice of translations: 'But now evil Ravening Hunger sits in his eyes' and

---

[1] Cf. Theocr. 26. 27 ff. An explanation of this difficult passage (which is clear for the point which concerns us) is essayed by J. Carrière, *Pallas* 6 (1958), 7-19. Cf. also H. 3. 136-7.

[2] Cf. Dem. *De Cor.* 287, *Meid.* 118; Antiph. 5. 11. Also the language of the Cnidian *tabellae defixionum*, Collitz III, i. 3545, comparing nos. 3536 b, 3537, 3540, 3546. Hor. *Carm.* 3. 2. 26 ff. is very much to the point: uetabo, qui Cereris sacrum | uulgarit arcanae, *sub isdem* | *sit trabibus* fragilemque mecum | soluat phaselon.

[3] To appropriate Prof. Rose's thought, '*i.e.* it may at any moment turn τοιχώρυχος'.

'*But now evil Ravening Hunger sits before my eyes*'. The former has all the force of tradition behind it—the localization of various qualities: scorn on the nostrils, grace, beauty, shame, fear in the eyes, love on the heart, anger on the liver, pallor and fear on the cheek, and so on. A close parallel such as Theocr. 1. 18 would seem to clinch the matter: καί οἱ ἀεὶ δριμεῖα χολὰ ποτὶ ῥινὶ κάθηται. We may then imagine with Wilamowitz, that Kallimachos' contribution to the conceit was a new installation of hunger in the eyes, the look of craving which no one who has tended a child with gastro-enteritis and acute dehydration can easily forget. *But the poet is as mischievous as ever*. Erysichthon is now Ravening Hunger Incarnate, and Meineke, Schneider, Mair and Cahen [1] were right to adopt the second translation. In H. 6 Kallimachos does not waste an opportunity to utilize the comic, and if he can do so to our discomfiture, the more praise to him.

Erysichthon is a comic subject, the counterpart of Herakles in appetite, and an abstraction, Ravening Hunger. But, of course, not all the time, but progressively. Here we notice the representative of the two levels of reference which insinuate themselves into parts of Hymns 1, 2 and 5. Since the other two 'epiphany' hymns are represented, it would be surprising if H. 6 was completely different in this regard. Yet it is different, for we have no fusion of the Kalathos and Demeter—the basket has not the associations of a statue, and line 129 makes it plain that the goddess is really in her temple. No, the two levels of reference are transferred to the cautionary tale; at one moment Erysichthon is himself, at another Ravening Hunger.

These considerations seem to me to justify our seeing Doric comedy, and more especially Epicharmos, as the inspiration for Kallimachos' treatment of Erysichthon. There are two further points of interest, but we must tread carefully, for they owe something to an *argumentum a silentio* (or, more properly, an *argumentum a susurro*) and a belief that the fragments which have survived by accident are typical of the whole corpus. Firstly, the tone. 'The phallus, the indecency, the personal scurrility ... are entirely lacking', remarks Miss Lever (p. 52). Pickard-Cambridge (p. 407) would regard such a statement as overconfident. But there is reason to believe that Epicharmos' comedy, with its keen interest

---

[1] The last mentioned in the Budé edition, but not in his commentary on the Hymns.

in philosophic movements, was aimed at a more educated audience, and that the earthiness of Doric farce would in general have been eschewed. This would mean that Kallimachos had available a Doric comedy with a tone sufficiently elevated to appeal to him and his circle.

Secondly, 'political problems and important contemporaries are rarely mentioned' (Lever, p. 53). There are examples [1], but very few. If the fewness is typical, we may readily explain it in terms of the dangers that would attend upon comic satire of the Aristophanic type under a tyranny. Pindar could hymn Hiero, but Epicharmos might well have found it wise to keep largely to fiction. Now it has been rather disconcerting to some scholars that in Hs. 5 and 6 we do not find allusions to the Ptolemies or to contemporary history. We have mercifully laid aside the explanation which Susemihl once gave, that this absence of allusion to affairs of the court proved that the hymns were written during the poet's early period as an insignificant schoolmaster. But as late as 1938 Prof. Vollgraff [2] believed that there was a sufficient clue in the relations between Ptolemy and Argos from 278 to 272, to date H. 5 in that period. I fear that such efforts will always be wasted for these two hymns. The reason for the absence of allusion to contemporary affairs, I suggest, is that Kallimachos is reviving, within a hymnal framework, two literary forms, Doric threnodic elegy and Doric comedy. The chances are that neither form had a pronounced interest in contemporary things, and so they are absent from Kallimachos. In any case, he would have been unwise to distract the reader by such complicating side issues.

It may be suggested that a simple opposition of tragedy (traced by some ancients to the Dorians) and comedy is intended, rather than the more specific threnody. To be sure, the poet uses many dramatic techniques, but a subject for threnody lends itself to such a treatment. Moreover, the type of comedy which I envisage is as specific as the threnody. One could not say simply 'tragedy', unless Doric tragedy had a specific form, which could be detected in H. 5. The idea of Doric threnodic elegy also accounts for the metre. If tragedy were involved, we would have to find a good reason for the elegiacs, which would, at the same time, differentiate this

---

[1] See Pickard-Cambridge, pp. 381, 408.
[2] *Bull. de l'Acad. royale de Belgique*, pp. 34 ff.

type of elegiac compos'tion from the narrative elegy to which Kallimachos' audience was attuned.

If the metre of H. 5 is taken from the Doric type, it may be asked why the poet has not used Epicharmos' characteristic metres. I imagine it was because of the contrasting tones of the two stories with which he was concerned. That is to say, the crushing of Erysichthon is in the epic manner, and suggested to him that he turn the normal epic hexameter to good effect in a Doric dress. Kallimachos has made no attempt to import local colour into his use of Doric. As we have seen, it was not his practice to use a dialect which could be localized, even in a literary sense. Hence it is of no importance that Epicharmos used πωλύ, not πουλύ (H. 6.2), and μόνος, not μοῦνος/μῶνος (H. 6.8) or, conversely, that he uses accusatives plural in -ὸς and -ἄς (Pickard-Cambridge, p. 408 n. 7; cf. H. 6.34 ἀρχίος). I mention this point because Cahen [1] uses it as evidence against the view that Kallimachos wrote in literary Syracusan; there may be some disposed to transfer the argument against Epicharmos. One would only need to point out that H. 5, for all its obvious associations with Argos, cannot be shown to involve a peculiarly Argive variety of Doric.

When the tension of fasting is removed, a reaction of uninhibited and riotous relief is to be expected. For this the burlesque is, dramatically speaking, admirably suited. If I am right, Howald-Staiger (p. 150) are far from the truth when they follow mention of humorous elements in the Erysichthon story with the caution: 'But we dare to laugh only on the sly, so deeply conscious are we of the presence of divinity'. There is no conflict at any level between the proximity of the Kalathos and the feeling of euphoria abroad among Demeter's devotees. We must expect a powerful reaction from the release of pent up emotions; moreover, Demeter is a divinity whose worship was by no means free from scurrility, even at her major festivals. In fact we have in this hymn an illustration of Kallimachos' mastery over his material which fills me with deep respect. It concerns the role of Hesperos at lines 7 ff.

We mentioned earlier in this chapter that Hesperos is given mythological status by the poet. The *time* of Demeter's breaking of her fast is treated, in the person of Hesperos, as the *reason* for it. We also mentioned that in such a role Hesperos replaces Iambe of the canonical myth. Let us remember the part played by Iambe.

---

[1] *Callimaque*, p. 435.

Demeter sat silent, unsmiling, fasting, 'until true-hearted Iambe *with many a joke moved the holy lady to smile and laugh and cheer her heart'* [1]). We can now see the complete groundplan:

MOURNING DEMETER (*Threnody*)
    is changed by HESPEROS (*Iambe*)
        into LAUGHING DEMETER (*Comedy*).

The poet himself has clarified his purposes in Hs. 5 and 6.

Realization of this should change our entire approach to H. 6. By way of example. It is rather unfortunate that the opening mention of Erysichthon is incomplete: 'Better <to tell> how (so that one may avoid transgressions) π............. ἰδέσθαι '(22-3). Clearly there is a reference to Demeter's treatment of the House of Triopas, but that the end of line 23 is something like <οἰκτρὸν> ἰδέσθαι is far from certain. Kallimachos may as easily have come out into the open. The missing idea may be 'ridiculous', 'comic', γελοῖον or the like [2].

In my later study I shall seek to throw light upon the poet's sense of the comic. Here I shall lay the foundation by noting that, if H. 5 is a combination of special form (threnody) and story illuminated by a highly individual approach (namely the use of Athene Oxyderkes), then we may expect H. 6 to feature, besides special form (comedy), a story on which no less time has been spent in arrangement of detail. The obstruction to earlier successful analysis of these two hymns, I suspect, has been the fact that they give an impression of sufficiency at the level of casual reading. This is hardly surprising, in view of the attention which the poet has shown to the outward form. But he was writing for a circle which was keenly alive to the force of innuendo, literary reminiscence or learned reference. Part of the game was to satisfy such perceptivity, part also to see what subtle moves could escape their attention. There are all of these things in the treatment of the Erysichthon story, and nice attention to the details of the tale itself. But that is another story.

---

[1] *Hom. Hymn. Dem.* 202-5. See Allen-Halliday ad *Dem.* 195.

[2] In Philikos' Hymn to Demeter (line 8, Page, *Greek Literary Papyri*, p. 406) Iambe's banter is preceded by τοῖσι δὲ]σεμνοῖς ὁ γελοῖος λόγος ἄρ' ἀκερδή[ς;

EPILOGUE

What exactly has Kallimachos accomplished in H. 5? In the space of some 140 lines he has infused new life into a conventional subject (Teiresias' blinding), purified and justified a crude version (Pherekydes), either invented or set a seal of approval upon a new treatment of Aktaion, invigorated a conventional form (the hymn), and revived an ancient type of composition (Doric threnodic elegy) in appropriate dialect. If we add to these the possibility of literary criticism, we find that the poem is far more complicated than a casual reading suggests. Although ingredients differ, this is no less true of Hymn 6. Whether it is true of every poem I do not know; the proof, alas, may be in the solving. For this reason in Chapter I I resisted the temptation to describe, for example, Hymn 3 as 'a rather tame epyllion'; such labels imply that we understand the poet's purpose.

I think it is worth asking whether we find in antiquity a parallel for Kallimachos. I am sure that we do. Although it was Propertius who laid claim to the title of Roman Kallimachos, it is the Vergil of the *Eclogues* who catches the spirit of the Callimachean hymn. I close with a few random thoughts on this subject, in the hope that others may be able to carry it further. Perhaps I shall find it already done in Dr. Walter Wimmel's forthcoming *Kallimachos in Rom*.

The fact that Vergil is indebted to Theokritos for the form of the Pastoral, for the interplay of shepherd and poet, and for many reminiscences which give overtones to Vergil's verse, has naturally led writers to think of him as the Roman Theokritos [1] and to devote little thought to the poet of Cyrene. To be sure, direct reference seems to occur only twice. In the sixth eclogue the literary manifesto of Kallimachos (fr. 1.21-24) is also revealed by Apollo to Vergil:

> Cum canerem reges et proelia, Cynthius aurem
> uellit et admonuit: 'pastorem, Tityre, pingues
> pascere oportet oues, deductum dicere carmen.

---

[1] E. g. E. V. Rieu, *Virgil, The Pastoral Poems* (Penguin Classics 1949), p. 12.

But since Horace, Propertius and Ovid also claimed the same
vision [1], this is not a special case. In the ninth eclogue Kallimachos'
memorable epigram on the death of Herakleitos of Halikarnassos
(Epigr. 2) adds overtones of pathos to lines 51-3:

> Omnia fert aetas, animum quoque; saepe ego longos
> cantando puerum memini me condere soles:
> nunc oblita mihi tot carmina.

But the influence of Kallimachos runs deeper than mere verbal
echo. It is only in Kallimachos that we find the kaleidoscopic
complexity of the Vergilian eclogue—literary allusion, literary
criticism, reference to contemporary politics, clever attention to
the paradox, riddle and playful humour, coupled with concern
for form, metre and sound. In the second eclogue, for example,
which has something of 'a Walter Mitty complexion' (a happy
thought of Prof. J. R. Trevaskis of Adelaide University), we find
the two levels of reference which we have met in Hymns 1 (Zeus/
Philadelphos), 2 (Apollo/Philadelphos or Euergetes), 5 (Palladion/
Athene) and 6 (Erysichthon/Ravening Hunger). The subject is at
the same time Corydon the shepherd and, when he suffers delusions
of grandeur in his daydreaming, Theokritos' Cyclops, Polyphe-
mos. [2] All this, as it has been nicely expressed, represents Vergil
in 'undergraduate' mood, playing upon a new form, the Pastoral,
as Kallimachos played upon an old form, the Hymn. Perhaps
Rieu [3] is right in interpreting the oft discussed *molle atque facetum*
of Horace's assessment of the poetry of the Eclogues as 'tender
and playful'. If he is right, it is worth recalling that we have been
studying a poet who has a pre-eminent claim to the second adjective
at least.

Needless to say, it still stands that the difference makes all
the difference. Already in the Eclogues Vergil shows a sensitivity
to the problems and meaning of life, whereas the brilliance of the
Hellenist never seems to have been prompted by deeper purpose
than self-satisfaction or self-commendation. Vergil realized that
he must outgrow the stage of the Poet at Play. He says as much
in the closing lines of the tenth eclogue, lines which give the im-

---

[1]   Hor. *Carm.* iv. 15, 1 ff.; *Sat.* II 6, 14 f. (cf. *Sat.* I 10, 31 ff.); Prop. IV.
1, 131 ff. (cf. Call. fr. 1. 20); III 3, 13 ff.; Ov. *Ars amat.* II 493 ff.
[2]   See H. J. Rose, *The Eclogues of Vergil* (1942), pp. 34, 35, 38.
[3]   *Op. cit.* p. 11.

pression of having been designed to serve as an *envoi* to the whole collection:

> Surgamus: solet esse grauis cantantibus *umbra*,
> iuniperi grauis *umbra*, nocent et frugibus *umbrae*.

ite domum saturae, uenit Hesperus, ite capellae. (75-7). I have not encountered an adequate comment on these lines, and as I have looked in vain for it in Marie Desport's veritable encyclopedia on the Pastoral, *L'Incantation Virgilienne* (Bordeaux 1952), a few remarks on *umbra* as a pastoral motif are in order.

Otium is one of the necessary conditions of the *ludus poeticus* [1]. In Vergil's Eclogues the ludus of the shepherd-poet is performed upon a rustic pipe in the shade. The heat of day provides the opportunity for leisure, and shade is an association of the latter. At Ecl. 1.4 Tityrus pipes *lentus in umbra*, courting the coolness of the shade (52), while Meliboeus is active. At 7.10 Meliboeus is invited by Daphnis to stop work, *requiesce sub umbra* and listen to song. At 5.3-7 Menalcas and Mopsus look for shade for their piping and song. By way of contrast, there is special effect in Ecl. 2, where shade and song give place to heat and song in Corydon's distraction.

In the tenth eclogue the shepherd-poet has continued his playing until a very late hour. The references to the tradition that the shade of certain trees was dangerous (cf. Lucr. 6.783), and to the obvious fact that crops dislike shade, are, I suspect, reminders of the ambivalence of shade. The variety which serves as a motif for Vergil's clever pastoral verse is pleasant; it provides escape, and the opportunity for a literary frolic. But when sojourn beneath it is prolonged, then it induces inertia and stagnation, the *frigida noctis umbra* (8.14). Pliny's words are appropriate, although he applies them to trees [2]: 'satis quibusque umbra aut nutrix aut nouerca est'. Vergil knows that he must leave the shade of clever, but essentially frivolous, pastoral poetry; he, like his goats, has had his fill. Now the more active, more purposive poetry of the *Georgics* and *Aeneid*.

Not that he will forget the lessons that he has learned, but they

---

[1] H. Wagenvoort, *Études Classiques* 4 (1935), 108-120 = *Studies in Roman lit., Culture and Religion* (Leiden 1956), 30-42; M. Desport, *op. cit.,* p. 128; J. Bayet, *L'influence grecque etc.* (Fondation Hardt II, 1956), 17 ff.

[2] *Nat. Hist.* XVII. xii. 18.

will be turned to advantage upon a worthier theme. I take two examples at random, from Aeneid IV. In the description of Atlas at lines 246-251 we find a magnificent Hellenistic fusion of images. We start with the mountain and end with the figure of mythology. To more than one modern editor it is not a fusion, but a confusion of images. When it is put against its proper background, and also related to its function (to relieve the tension of the previous scene), I have been happy to find that students dissent from that verdict.

Of rather more interest is line 108. Juno suggests to Venus that they settle their differences and allow Aeneas and Dido to marry. Vergil makes it quite clear that Venus is fully aware of Juno's ulterior motive: 'sensit enim simulata mente locutam, quo regnum Italiae Libycas auerteret oras' (105-6). She starts her reply: 'quis talia demens. .'. *Demens* is a strong word, suggestive of a forceful retort to come. 'A plan like that what woman would be mad enough to . .' What do we expect? Surely 'accept', *accipiat* or the like. It is the answer which Juno, despite her attempt to hoodwink Venus, should anticipate from her canny rival. But Vergil's Venus 'plays along', making it plain by an unexpected verb that she is wide awake to the manoeuvre, but that it suits her purpose to allow Aeneas an affair in Carthage. The poet leaves us to reconstruct the concomitant moods- Venus' straight face at *quis talia demens*, the saccharine smile at the unexpected *abnuat*. The entire verbal sparring is delightful; Callimachean mischief at its best.

So Vergil went home, but Kallimachos was content to linger in the shade.

SHORT LIST OF RECOMMENDED READING

This list features only the most useful of the works that I have consulted. I have deliberately refrained from listing items which I have had no chance to evaluate; hence the omission, for example, of F. Dornseiff's *Die Mythische Erzählung* (1933). If I mention that Cahen's commentary on the Hymns was loaned by the University of Dijon, the reader may gauge the difficulties under which scholarship is undertaken in Australia.

For a detailed survey of the literature on Kallimachos between 1921 and 1935 we have H. Herter in Bursians Jahresbericht, 255 (1937). The same author provides a bibliography in *R.E.* Suppbd. v (1931), 436. 452. A more general survey of Hellenistic literature will be found in *Fifty Years of Classical Scholarship* (ed. Platnauer, 1954), pp. 214-232 (written by E. A. Barber). For the editions of Mair, Cahen, Ardizzoni, Pfeiffer and Howald-Staiger, see the Preface of my study.

Special mention should be made of the very sane and readable account of Kallimachos in Albin Lesky's *Geschichte der griechischen Literatur* (Francke Verlag, Berne 1957/8), pp. 638-655.

Hellenistic Poetry:

C. A. Trypanis, 'The Character of Alexandrian Poetry', *Greece and Rome* 16 (1947), 1-7.

E. A. Barber, Cambridge Ancient History VII (1928), 249-283 (Bibliography, pp. 904 ff.).

A. Körte, *Hellenistische Dichtung* (Leipzig, 1925). Eng. trans. *Hellenistic Poetry* (J. Hammer-M. Hadas, Columbia Univ. Press, 1929).

Ph.-E. Legrand, *La Poésie Alexandrine* (Paris, 1924).

A. Couat, *La Poésie Alexandrine* (Paris, 1882). Eng. trans. *Hellenistic Poetry under the Three First Ptolemies, 324-222 B.C.* (J. Loeb, London 1931. It contains a supplementary chapter by E. Cahen).

Kallimachos and the Hymns:

E. Cahen, *Callimaque et son oeuvre poétique* (Paris, 1929).

E. Cahen, *Les hymnes de Callimaque* (Paris, 1930).

E. Howald, *Der Dichter Kallimachos von Kyrene* (Zürich, 1943).

U. von Wilamowitz-Moellendorff, *Hellenistische Dichtung in der Zeit des Kallimachos*, vol. II (Berlin, 1924).

H. Kleinknecht, ΛΟΥΤΡΑ ΤΗΣ ΠΑΛΛΑΔΟΣ, *Herm.* 74 (1939), 301-350.

Useful literature on special points:

Ph.-E. Legrand, 'Pourquoi furent composés les Hymnes de Callimaque?', *R.E.A.* 3 (1901), 281-312.

B. A. van Groningen, *La poésie verbale grecque*, (Mededelingen der K. Nederlandse Akad. van Wetenschappen, Afd. Letterkunde, 16, 4 (Amsterdam, 1953).

C. del Grande, *Filologia Minore* (Milan/Naples, 1956), ch. 23, pp. 231-264 'Espressione Callimachea e Tradizione di Forma Lirica'.

K. Ziegler, 'Kallimachos und die Frauen', *Die Antike* 13 (1937), 20-42.

H. Erbse, 'Zum Apollonhymnos des Kallimachos', *Herm.* 83 (1955), 411-428.

B. Snell, Die Entdeckung des Geistes[3] (Hamburg, 1955), pp. 353-370: 'Über das Spielerische bei Kallimachos'. (Eng. trans. *The Discovery of the Mind* [T. G. Rosenmeyer, Oxford 1953], pp. 264-280: 'Art and Play in Callimachus'.)

ADDENDA AND CORRIGENDA

I feel a certain dissatisfaction with Chapter I. It should have been much longer, with a large section on duality, drawing on the multitude of examples in H. 4 (e.g. the identification of places and their eponyms); the more so as the best pages on the subject that I know are in Dutch (J. C. Arens, *De Godenschildering in Ovidius' Metamorphosen*, Diss. Nijmegen 1946, pp. 28 ff., 178 ff.). I shall try to rectify this omission in a following study of Hymns 6 and 4. Another cause of discontent was my inability, when writing the chapter, to keep it in step with a sequence of lucky breaks; hence parts of it still illustrate the indecision which preceded reaching a firm conclusion for H. 2. *Viresque acquirit eundo.* H. 4 has now capitulated, and proves—with scant respect for my intuition (p. 24)—to be subsequent to H. 2; Prof. Von der Mühll had reached a similar conclusion but our reasons are quite different. I cannot expect scholars who work on Apollonios of Rhodes to receive this idea with wild delight, but I believe that a precious byproduct of this new advance is the assurance that the subject of H. 2 is Philadelphos.

P. 14 n.   For ἐπί as 'in the case of' see especially A. Mauersberger, *Polybios-Lexikon*, col. 882 *s.v.*

P. 18.   Some pertinent remarks on Pindar's use of *mastos* in his imagery will be found in S. L. Radt, *Pindars Zweiter und Sechster Paian*, Diss. Amsterdam 1958, 182 f. I should also have mentioned Archestratos ap. Athen. 111f, cited by Cahen (*Comm.*, p. 165): ἐν Λέσβῳ κλεινῆς Ἐρέσου περικύμονι μαστῷ.

P. 21.   Bowra (*Greek Poetry and Life* (Essays Gilbert Murray 1936), p. 334 = *Problems in Greek Poetry*, p. 160) supports the second thoughts of Blass, that Erinna is the authoress of *P. Oxy.* I. 8.

P. 36.   J. Schwartz, *Pseudo-Hesiodeia* (Leiden 1960), pp. 213 n. 5 and 218 n. 2, discusses a gesture made by Hera which may have been part of the *Hesiodic* story of Teiresias' blinding. Hyginus (*fab.* 75. 3) says 'manu auersa eum excaecauit'; Phlegon (257 F 36 Jacoby) is much more direct: τὴν δὲ Ἥραν ὀργισθεῖσαν κατανύξαι αὐτοῦ τοὺς ὀφθαλμοὺς καὶ ποιῆσαι τυφλόν. I cannot agree with Schwartz that κατανύξαι means 'frapper' (it is surely 'jab', 'stab'), while when he brings the ταῖς χερσί of pseudo-Apollodoros into the picture, he forgets that this is the Pherecydean version, involving Athene, not Hera. The sources for Hera's gesture do not inspire confidence.

P. 42 n. 2.   I should not have robbed J. T. Allen of his greater share in the index to Euripides which he compiled with assistance from G. Italie.

P. 45.   For the manner in which Teiresias and Aktaion are opposed J. C. Arens (*De Godenschildering in Ovidius' Metamorphosen*, 1946, p. 70) is worth reading. He also remarks that Nonnos, remembering Kallimachos, makes Athene οἰκτίρμων (5.338), but Artemis βαρύφρων (5.327).

P. 54.   On Teiresias see also Robert, *Gr. Heldensage* I (1920), pp. 127-130. It is not true to say (p. 129 n. 2) that when Phlegon declares that Kallimachos used the Hesiodic version, he refers to H. 5.128 ff.

P. 57 n.3. Cf. W. Bühler *ad* Mosch. *Europa* 97/98 (p. 144). I wonder now whether we should not respect the received text of Mnasalkes *Anth. Pal.* 9.324.1 (ἀ σῦριγξ τί τυ κτλ.) as imitative of the subject. The text is emended by Wilamowitz, Stadtmueller and Paton, but preserved by Beckby (1958). Dr. Bühler doubts whether Prof. Van Groningen's interpretation of the line in Moschos is really appropriate to a Phrygian mode, but Call. H. 3. 242-3 gives us a useful picture of the general impression made by the tone of the σῦριγξ: ὑπήεισαν δὲ λίγειαι/λεπταλέον σύριγγες.

P. 62.   For heroes as stars cf. Ap. Rhod. I, 240, 774; II. 41.

P. 71.   F. Vian, *La Guerre des Géants*, 1952, pp. 260, 266-7, has some good comments on the warlike aspects of Athene.

P. 91.   To the literature on Epigr. 2 should now be added B. Snell, *Glotta* 37 (1958), 1-4.

P. 98.   I should have compared Eur. *Med.* 1207f. ὦ δύστηνε παῖ, / τίς σ' ὧδ' ἀτίμως δαιμόνων ἀπώλεσε;

P. 112.   In connexion with H. 6. 13 ff. perhaps the verdicts of Cahen (*Comm.*, pp. 257-8) deserve at least to be recorded: the triple circuit of the earth is seen as 'des détails d'ornement où figure le nombre parfait', while the use of Kallichoron shows only poetic *insouciance*.

P. 125.   Dr. Wimmel's study led him along quite a different track, and my expectation was not satisfied. His contribution to the literature on H. 2 will have to be examined later.

P. 129.   To the bibliography must now be added the revision of Alfred Körte's *Die hellenistische Dichtung* by Paul Händel (Kröner Verlag: Stuttgart 1960). H. 5 is handled on pp. 46-50, H. 6 on pp. 50-53, but, in common with much in the book, the treatment here is disappointing.

INDICES

AUCTORUM RECENTIUM

INDEX LOCORUM

.137	57LF	.95	76L
.139	57LF	.97	76L
.139f.	87S	.102	120P
.140f.	57LF	.105	20L
.141f.	59F	.113	20L
6	58, 106 ff.	.116	49FP
.1	110S	.116f.	51f.F, 119f.FP
.2	123L	.117	50FP
.3	110S	.118-133	114FP
.5	110S	.120 ff.	101E
.6	110S	.125	76L
.7 ff.	108P, 123f.P	.126f.	52FP, 102FP
.8	123L	.127f.	115nF
.9	110S	Epigr. 2	
.10	110S	.1f.	97, 126
.13 ff.	111 ff.P	16.4	94
.14	110S	19(21)	92
.15	111S	44.2	91
.17	97S, 110S	Frag. 1.19f.	15n
.22f.	124F	.21-24	125
.25 ff.	93E	55.2	61, 95
.29f.	37P	67.8	62
.33	76L	75	85
.34	123L	114	50
.38	116FE	177.5f.	108
.39	85S	203.18	77
.41	97S	227	58n
.46-9	116P	260.41	71
.53	40	.52	95
.59	40F	.53	89
.63f.	116P	.67f.	89
.65	104F	398	103
.66f.	119L	576	54
.67	76L, 120L	611	112
.73	99P	676.1	42
.77	94L	Schol. H. 5.1 ff.	27, 69
.83	99E	.37	67
.94f.	20P, 117P		

INDEX RERUM ET NOMINUM

Achaios 117
Aeschylus 89
Aithon 119
Aktaion 27, 39, 45 ff.
Alkaios 22 ff.
Antimachos 78, 102 ff.
Apollo 15, 23
— Delios 50
— Karneios 16
Apollodoros 35f.
Argos 30
Arsinoe 17, 78n

Artemis 22, 38n
Athene 26 ff., 43 ff., 55 ff., 62 ff., 116
   Birth of, 53f.
— Akria 28, 70
— Alalkomeneis 54
— Aposkopousa? 31
— Hippia 59
— Ophthalmitis 29
— Optilitis 29
— Oxyderkes 28 ff., 34f., 42, 54, 64, 67, 68f., 70, 75, 107, 124

INDEX VERBORUM GRAECORUM